Alfred B Westrup

The New Philosophy of Money

A practical treatise on the nature and office of money and the correct method of its

supply

Alfred B Westrup

The New Philosophy of Money
A practical treatise on the nature and office of money and the correct method of its supply

ISBN/EAN: 9783337236618

Printed in Europe, USA, Canada, Australia, Japan

Cover: Foto ©Suzi / pixelio.de

More available books at **www.hansebooks.com**

Alfred B. Westrup

THE NEW PHILOSOPHY
OF MONEY

A PRACTICAL TREATISE ON THE NATURE
AND OFFICE OF MONEY
AND THE CORRECT METHOD OF ITS SUPPLY

BY

ALFRED B. WESTRUP

Author of "The Financial Problem" and "Citizens' Money"

MINNEAPOLIS
IDEAL PUBLISHER
1895

CONTENTS.

NOTE—The figures in parenthesis throughout this work are for the purpose of calling attention to the paragraph of that number.

PREFACE.

This work is an investigation as to the nature and office of money; what constitutes the most satisfactory money, and the best method of providing for its supply. It is necessarily, therefore, an exposition of the errors and fallacies that are accountable for the prevailing unsound notions and the apparently inextricable confusion that characterize the subject, and are responsible for the existing absurd money systems.

The title, The New Philosophy of Money, might, perhaps, better have been formulated, The Philosophy of Money. Putting it in this positive form affirms that which it claims to be—the correct and only sound theory of money. *A* philosophy may be knowledge imperfectly understood, and contain errors, but *the* philosophy of a subject should be knowledge which has been demonstrated. It should be complete, and so formulated that all error is excluded. The New Philosophy of Money has been adopted as the title, for, while it is an old subject, the philosophy here presented is not only correct, but it is new.

The reader will find herein treated all the facts and theories that have a bearing on the subject, including that diplomatic phase of it called "finance."

Heretofore, the end that should have been sought—a faultless medium of exchange—has been lost sight of; and every writer who has presented a new theory of money, not to mention the old one, has become entangled with the dogmas, State supervision, "measure of value," "standard of value," and legal tender; or lost his bearings and shipwrecked among the breakers—fiat money, wildcat money, monometallism, bimetallism, and the like.

Production and exchange being the two great burdens that the constitution of things imposes on us, exchange being fully as important as production (because if exchange stops, production must stop also), and a medium of exchange, *called money*, being indispensable to the accomplishment of exchange, *what* money will the most effectually and economically fulfil its office, and how to provide it, is a question of the very first magnitude, if it does not transcend all others. If the invention of an instrument used in the production of only one article of the thousands that contribute to comfort is of value to mankind, how much more so is that instrument which enables us to exchange all those products, and without which we could not enjoy them because we could not possess them? On this question of the best medium of exchange there is absolutely no conflict of interest. If it is reliable and there is enough of it, all are benefited; no one can be hurt by it. If it is unreliable, all are involved in the risk, and all interests are damaged.

This is the ground on which The New Philosophy of Money appeals to the reader in behalf of the Mutual Credit System. The writer makes no pretensions to originality or special merit. Whatever new idea, term, or definition may be presented here for the first time, he will, no doubt, in due time get credit for. The allusion to its being new has reference to the manner of presenting it; and that, in the popular sense, it is new.

With grateful remembrance, the author acknowledges his indebtedness to the writings of Col. Wm. B. Greene, E. H. Heywood, Josiah Warren, and others.

THE AUTHOR.

INTRODUCTION.

1 "The money question" is a title applied to that subject which is a philosophical inquiry into the nature and office of money, and necessarily includes an investigation as to how it originates, what are the methods employed in making it and furnishing the supply; and, finally, the maturing of a plan that shall correct any defects that may be discovered in those methods.

2 The terms "money" and "medium of exchange" are applied to that instrument which is used to facilitate the exchange of objects of value, and which is not the direct exchange of objects without the intervention of money; this latter kind of exchange being known by the term "barter" (81, 88).

3 It does not matter what this instrument or medium of exchange is composed of. It is not the quality of the instrument that entitles it to be called money, but whether it performs, in a general way, the office or function of money. There has been a very great variety of money, and there are many kinds of money now in use throughout the world, and some of it is very poor money; but to say that only a certain kind is money, and that all others are only substitutes for money, is a play upon words and does not conduce to a more intelligent understanding of the question.

4 There must be a general term by which we can designate the various instruments that perform the function of money. "Money" has always been and is used in this sense. Among other definitions given in the Century Dictionary we find: "Any circulating medium of exchange."

5   There are instruments that perform in a limited way
the function of money, but which are not called money.
For instance: a check on a bank, a promissory note, a bill of
exchange or draft, fulfil the office of money in at least one
instance, but they do not circulate generally, and it is for
this reason that the term money is not applied to them.

6   As to what is good, and what bad money, depends
upon whether it circulates generally without liability of
incurring loss to anyone; but this is only one of the important items.   In the supply of money, we have to deal with
quantity (volume) as well as quality.   The supply must
not only consist of good money, but there must be enough of
it (46); and this is the item that all other theories of money
have failed to resolve—what constitutes enough—notwithstanding it can be as satisfactorily answered as the questions, how many square inches in a given area, or how long
it would take for a calf to become a year old.   It is not that
the problem is so difficult to solve, but that the investigation
has not been pursued fearlessly and with a determination to
arrive at the truth.   It is very evident that there must be
some natural limit to the volume of money (14), just as there
is a natural limit to all material things, and when we have
determined correctly what that natural limit is, we shall be
very much nearer the solution as to how much is enough (35).

7   We have already learned that the office or function of
money is to facilitate the exchange of products; but to pursue our investigation, to determine what is the natural limit
to the volume, we must also know the nature of money.

8   The nature of money depends upon the product or
commodity of which it is made.   To illustrate: The market value of the commodity of which coin is made constitutes a large percentage of the face value of the coin, while
the market value of the commodity that bank-notes, or bills,
or treasury notes are made of, is but an infinitesimal fraction
of their face value.   The nature of coin money, then, is different from that of paper money; and we may designate

coin as commodity money, and paper money as credit money; for paper money is really a form of credit (9). Now, the natural limit to the volume of commodity money is very easy to determine. The limit is arbitrary. The metal of which it is made is found only in limited quantities, and there is no way of adding to it. But it is not so with the material of which paper money is made. It is practically without limit. The supply of the volume, therefore, however large it may be desirable to have it, will not be hampered by scarcity of the material to make it of.

9   If it is not limited like commodity money, and if our definition relative to its nature is correct, then it is as such that we must deal with it. We must determine its limit as a form of credit; but as there is more than one form of credit, we must state wherein they differ. There are two forms of credit (84-85); one is secured and the other unsecured (86). Book accounts or time credits are generally unsecured credits. A simple promissory note is unsecured credit, while a mortgage note is secured credit. Paper money is, or should be, secured credit. It is the credit of the party who issued it. For instance: "treasury notes" are the credit of the United States government. Gold certificates are the credit of the party who deposited the gold they are issued on; the same with silver certificates. Bank-notes are the credit of the bank that issued them, although they are not always secured.

10   We have now arrived at something definite as to the nature of money. The definitions given, namely: that coin money is commodity money and that paper money is secured credit, are strictly true of the best of each kind, and that is the only kind we can consider.

11   The task now before us is to find the natural limit to that form of secured credit called paper money. The question arises whether that which determines the natural limit in one form of secured credit determines the natural limit in

all forms. I have explained what is secured credit, but it
will be well to formulate a precise definition.

12   Secured credit is debt incurred with ample provision
made to insure payment (79-91).

13   Secured credit, then, originates in the voluntary acts
of two or more parties.   There must be at least one (there
may be more) who incurs the debt, and one or more to
whom the debt is incurred.   The other essentials are: The
material upon which the promise is recorded (paper) and
the security; and since, as we have seen, there is practically
no limit to the material (paper), the natural limit to secured
credit would seem to be determined by the security, because
it is the only thing that can limit it.   What difference, then,
does it make, whether it is a secured note, paper money, or
any other form?   It is the security that determines the natural limit to any form of secured credit.   Where there is no
security there can be no secured credit; where there is security, there can be.

14   We have now determined the natural limit to the
volume of money.   The natural limit to the volume of coin
money is the quantity of the metal of which it is made.
You can make as much gold coin as you can get gold bullion
to make it of.   You cannot make any more.   The natural
limit to the volume of paper money is security; the material
of which it is made being unlimited, you can make as much
paper money as you have security to convert the paper
promises to pay into secured credit, so that no one will run
any risk in taking them in exchange for commodities.

15   Remember, this is the *natural* limit; and it is perti-
nent to inquire now, what relation it bears to the question:
"how much is enough?"   It is evident that there can be no
more; but why should there be any less?   Our definition for
secured credit is, "debt incurred with ample provision made
to insure payment," and we have defined paper money to be
a form of secured credit.   It is not denied that an individual
has the right to incur debt, but he must not incur it in this

form without complying with certain restrictions.* Here we have an artificial limit; and our next inquiry must be to ascertain what is the object of this artificial limit.

16 I have already explained that the term "money" is applied to that instrument which is in general use for the purpose of facilitating the exchange of products, but this is not sufficiently definite. Its use in the cancellation of indebtedness and in payment for services, while it should not be omitted, is, in reality, but a part of exchange. It should be stated, also, that the use of money obviates the necessity for barter, and so expedites exchange, which would otherwise be hampered and even impossible. But do these statements include all the uses that money is put to and all the purposes it subserves? There can be no denying that to a money-lender, at least that portion of his money which he lends, serves him a purpose not included in those I have named. He does not use it himself for the purpose of exchange, but loans it to another who needs it for that purpose. The purpose of the money-lender is to derive an income from it. Here our field of inquiry widens. We are confronted with conflicting interests. We find that money is used for another and quite different purpose than that of facilitating exchange; and that the interest of the party using it for the one purpose is hostile to the interest of the party using it for the other purpose. For is it not to the interest of the money-lender, as such, that there be a scarcity of money and that the rate of interest be high? And is it not to the interest of borrowers that there be plenty of money and that interest be low? How could interest be low with a scarcity of money? Or how could interest be high with plenty of money? The scarcer money is, the greater the opportunity of the possessor to lend it; and the greater the demand for it, the higher the rate of interest.

---

*The restrictions here referred to are those which interfere with the free issue of paper money, such as the 10 per cent tax imposed by congress and the requirements in the different States.

17   To be sure that these interests are distinct and opposed to each other, let us pursue our investigation still further.

18   It is claimed that in this country all should have equal rights; and this ought to be especially true with regard to the supply of the medium of exchange. The means of obtaining it that are open to one should be open to all. Let us see if it is so.

19   The source of supply of money in this country is the United States government. It will coin gold for all on equal terms, or give gold certificates in exchange for gold bullion. But this is the only commodity it will now coin into money or upon which it will issue certificates.

20   Other paper money may be obtained by organizing national banks and depositing United States bonds in the United States treasury; but you must organize a bank. Such paper money cannot be procured by an individual borrower.

21   Here we have discrimination in favor of one commodity, and in favor of bankers and against those who are not. What becomes of this boast about equal rights? Money is loaned every day on every conceivable kind of security, from a piece of ordinary kitchen furniture to a private mansion or a block of buildings; a manufacturing plant, or an entire railroad; but all such money must go through the hands of money-lenders. Not one of these borrowers can get money from first source.

22   Now, the special claim that The New Philosophy of Money makes is, that paper money being secured credit, whoever can furnish the security is entitled to that form of credit; that equality of rights demands it, and that to deny it is to deny the right of private property.

23   But this is not all. It unqualifiedly affirms that it is of the very greatest importance; that it is to the very best interest of all concerned, including the money-lenders them-

selves, that this right be recognized at once, and that the plan that will make its realization possible be adopted.

24   But, before we proceed further into this labyrinth of inconsistencies and incoherencies called political economy, let us clear up as we go, and make sure our own position.

25   The questions still pending, of those brought to the notice of the reader, are: "What is the object of this artificial limit to paper money?" and, still farther back, is that all-important one, "how much is enough?"

26   I have pointed out that the means employed to bring about this artificial limit are legislative enactments by congress and State legislatures, that restrict the issue of paper money and furnish it to bankers only.

27   I have shown, also, that the rate of interest, like the price of commodities, is affected by supply and demand; that a scarcity of money makes interest high, just as a scarcity of any article that there is a demand for will cause the price of that article to be high.

28   It follows, therefore, that the only object of limiting paper money to less than the natural limit, is to keep up the rate of interest; and it follows also, that since it benefits money-lenders only (68), it must be their work. Borrowers would hardly spend their time in efforts to secure the passage of laws in opposition to their own interests.

29   We will now devote our attention to the other question that remains unanswered. The reader should bear in mind what has been said about the source of the supply of money, and how the borrower is cut off from that source and is compelled to patronize the money-lender; and also that we have defined paper money to be a form of credit.

30   Now, if a borrower borrows paper money of a money-lender, he obtains credit (9). Whose credit is it that he obtains? It must be the credit of the money-lender. It certainly cannot be his own credit. To be his own credit, the money would have to be issued to him direct on his own security, just as gold certificates are issued on gold. What

he has borrowed must be either gold certificates, silver certificates, treasury notes or national bank notes. They are not
his credit. They were issued by the government, not to
him, but to a money-lender, and he borrowed them of the
same or some other money-lender. But why should he use
the money-lender's credit? We must regard his security as
good. The money-lender would not lend his money on it if
it were not. If it is good enough to insure the return of
paper money that is redeemable in gold, it must be equivalent to gold; if it is good enough to secure such money it
must be as good as gold. If it is as good as gold, why not
issue certificates on it just as well as on gold? Again I ask:
Why should he use the money-lender's credit when his
security is as good as gold? Is he not deprived of his right
to the use of his property for purposes of credit? If he cannot use his property in this way without the consent of the
money-lender, then he is not the absolute owner of that
property. Is it not a denial of the right of private property?

31   Suppose a farmer, who owns a farm which is unen-
cumbered with debt, rents his farm and moves with his family into town. He has, besides his farm, considerable grain
in warehouse. He needs some household furniture, and
proceeds to investigate as to its cost. The furniture dealer
foots up the cost and it amounts to $500. The farmer asks
him how much he will discount it if he pays him C. O. D.
The dealer informs him that he will deduct 6 per cent if he
pays cash down on receipt of goods. The farmer has no
money, but he has good security. He has $2,000 worth of
grain, and he proceeds to inquire what it will cost him
to borrow the $500. He learns that a money-lender will
accommodate him at the rate of 6 per cent interest, holding
all his grain as security. Surely no one will claim that this
is not a fair illustration of present methods.

32   It makes no difference whether the $500 are bor-
rowed or whether the goods are bought on the usual two or

three months time.   In either case, there is 6 per cent interest to be paid in excess of the cash price.   It is interest on
the money borrowed, or it is interest on the deferred payment
for the goods.

33   It is a correct business rule that where you pay out
money, it must be for value received; but what does this
farmer get in exchange for this $30?   He is willing to relieve
the furniture dealer of all risk, by paying him cash on receipt
of goods, but it does not save him from the loss of this $30.
The individual who enables him to pay cash, and who
charges him the $30 (who, by the way, is quite moderate;
there are usually additional charges, commission, etc., which
bring up interest to about 8 or 10 per cent), furnishes him
with what?   Some printed pieces of paper, the actual cost of
which does not exceed one-half of one per cent.   He as-
sumes no risk, for the security is ample (95).   The charge,
therefore, covers nothing but the printed pieces of paper; for
that is all the farmer gets.

34   Now let us come back to the question as we left it
before we introduced the illustration.   The proposition was
advanced that whatever collateral is good enough to secure
paper money that is redeemable in gold, must necessarily be
as good as the gold it is redeemable in; and the question was
put: "If it is as good as gold, why not issue certificates on
it just as well as on gold?"   There is no reason why this
should not be done.   It would be opening to all the means
of obtaining credit in the form of paper money, that are now
open only to a few (18, 19, 20, 21).   It would be the con-
ceding of a right that is now denied—the right to that credit
without the intervention of money-lenders—the right which
The New Philosophy of Money teaches inheres in the right
of private property; and that the individual has as much
right to that form of credit called paper money as he has to
make a mortgage note.   His right to make a promissory note
and secure it by mortgage is not questioned.   His right to

2

credit in the form of paper money cannot be successfully disputed. It would be assailing the right of property.

35   We have now the solution to the question, "how much is enough?" It is easy. The reader must already have foreseen it. When the artificial limit has been removed and all who have security can obtain the representative paper money credit he is entitled to, and from its source—direct from the printing press—instead of from the money-lender, the demand will be supplied; and when that is supplied, there is enough; but so long as that is not supplied, how can there be enough?

THE GENERAL EFFECT OF THE ARTIFICIAL LIMIT TO THE VOLUME OF MONEY.

36 Let us consider for a moment what would be the result if a system of money such as is proposed in The New Philosophy of Money, were in actual operation (129).* Would not all who could furnish security take advantage of the low rate of interest, and borrow all they could? Especially as the certainty that the rate would not be higher in the future, and become a cormorant and swallow them up at no distant day, as it does now, would be too apparent to leave any doubt.

37 And what would be the consequence resulting from the people borrowing so much money? When an individual borrows money it is with the object of going into some new enterprise, extending one already established, or paying off some debt. In either case, he is adding to the general increase of trade. What is true in one instance must be true in all; therefore, the greater the amount of money borrowed, the greater the increase in trade.†

38 Now, if this is the general effect that results when there is *no* artificial limit (15), the exact opposite must be the result when there *is* an artificial limit. The general effect, therefore, of the artificial limit to the volume of money is paralysis and stagnation to trade; and the more restriction, the more stagnation.

---

*See Appendix for plan.

†The reader must bear in mind that under the system herein proposed, all money borrowed will be new money, and therefore an addition to the volume in circulation; whereas, under the existing system, the borrowing of money adds nothing to the volume; being merely the transfer of that much from one party to another.

39   Just as a man without tools is helpless and remains idle, so production and exchange must stop when the tool, money, is absent. And in proportion to its abundance, and the ease with which it can be obtained, will be the activity or inactivity of trade; just as a scarcity or plentiful supply of tools will retard or accelerate the work of the mechanic.

40   Who can tell the marvelous development we might have attained, if there had never been an artificial limit to the volume of money? So far, a medium of exchange pure and simple, has never been provided. The money power, or the combined interests of money-lenders, has ever succeeded in inducing the people to use the makeshift that suits its purpose. The medium that will best perform the function of exchange, must, of necessity, be provided by the borrowers themselves; for their interest being the direct opposite of that of the money-lenders (16), as such, it is not natural to expect that the latter will initiate a movement in opposition to what they regard as their interest. The question may well arise in the mind of the reader, especially if he (or she) be somewhat of a thinker,—"is this a natural state of society? Are those normal institutions which engender antagonisms, and tend to form classes with opposing interests?" Since the aim and end of life is common to all—the attainment of happiness—and since whatever facilitates and simplifies production and exchange tends to reduce burdens, and, therefore, to the attainment of happiness, the real interest of all is identical. Progress involves change; therefore, our institutions must change or they are not progressive. As all are interested in progress because all are interested in happiness, and as we cannot attain happiness unless we change—progress from our present unhappy condition—the real interest of one class is not opposed to that of any other; and if there is apparent conflict of interest, it is because some institutions which have outlived their usefulness, or have not yielded to the iconoclastic hand of evolution, still stand as barriers to progress and block the road to happiness. It is

their interest as money-lenders that prompts them to encourage and perpetuate an institution which limits the supply of money and keeps up a high rate of interest; while it is to their interest as members of a common humanity, that that institution should give place to a more progressive and useful one.   Which, then, of these two interests is paramount—the attainment of happiness on the part of a class, or the attainment of happiness on the part of mankind as a whole?

41   There can be no such thing as the attainment of happiness on the part of a class, as distinct from the whole, unless it be at the sacrifice of the rest; and the question here arises: Could such a condition be considered a state of happiness?   Can an individual be happy surrounded by people living in poverty, with the necessary accompanying evils, such as disease and crime; his health and that of his family and friends in danger from unhygienic conditions breeding contagious diseases, to say nothing of the insecurity from invasion of person and property?   Can such an individual be happy?   If he congratulates himself upon his happiness, it is because he is ignorant of another kind of a vastly superior quality, and it is because he does not realize what are his true interests, that his constant aim is to get rid of the burdens of life by shifting them onto others.   Having succeeded, he is happy; but he has only postponed the evil.   A day of reckoning must come.   These others also desire to get rid of the burdens.   They are of the same flesh and blood; and the greater the burdens, the greater the danger; both from the unhygienic conditions and from discontent. His real interests consist, not in shifting the burdens, thus increasing those that others have to bear, but in the discovery of the means of getting rid of them altogether.   If this is true, how is it that he does not act with that end in view?

42   The fact is that society as it is today is the outgrowth of ignorance.   Its institutions are such as class interests have reared for their own benefit.   The real interests of mankind have been lost sight of.   We have an arbitrary money sys-

tem which limits credit, and makes it possible for a few to
control it.   This control is a power that few comprehend.
The scarcity of money in consequence of the artificial limit,
makes high rates of interest.   As all surplus funds are
invested from year to year—the interest on investments one
year is reinvested the next—and as all capital successfully
engaged in business receives interest, which is again reinvested, it is not difficult to see that a very large amount is
compounded every year, the marvelous rapidity of increase
of which (130) accounts for our millionaires, and, necessarily, also, for our paupers.   It is evident, therefore, that the
artificial limit and an arbitrary money system were not
devised for the benefit of mankind, but in the interest of a
few.   These millionaires and the pauperization of the masses
would never have occurred if there had been no artificial
limit to the volume of money.   There would be no arbitrary
money system and therefore no limit to credit, except the
natural one, if there had been no artificial limit to the volume
of money.   Usury, or interest, will come to an end when the
artificial limit to the volume of money shall cease to exist.
The possibility of getting a living without labor, and, therefore at the expense of others, is the most vitiating factor in
our civilization; for, as long as it is possible, however remote
the probability, however few the number who attain the
coveted goal, it will be the one thing that will absorb attention; the one aim of life to which all energies will be bent;
and of course, those questions which are of interest to mankind at large are subordinated to this all-consuming struggle, this all-absorbing theme; the accumulation of wealth in
order to live on the interest it brings.   Take away the artificial limit to the volume of money, and the institutions
that this class have reared in their interest will be left without a foundation—the civilization that is based upon usury
will come to an end.

43   It is vitiating, because, as Proudhon says, "property

is robbery."*   It cannot exist on its just basis, which is labor; therefore, in its true sense, "property is impossible" (123), for usury not only absorbs all property, but there is ever a balance which can never be paid, as Mr. J. W. Bennett has so clearly shown in his powerful article, "The Cause of Financial Panics," in the March "Arena," 1894 (118-126).

44   The class that would perpetuate our money system, once called "specie basis," but which is being narrowed down to a "gold basis," by the exclusion of silver; the class that has reared our institutions,—the State, with its manifold devices for plunder—its army and its navy to enforce them, its armories, its bastiles and its gatling guns to strike terror into the minds of its opponents, and its courts to solemnize its acts and justify its course; the class that elect themselves to office to legislate and to preside; what does this class know about the real interests of mankind?   They not only do not study the subject, but they override with their money and their vulgarity, any who, being especially adapted, should dare to show up the evils which result from the course they are pursuing.

45   The rest of the people are too busy struggling under the burdens this class has shifted onto them, to be able to give special attention to the grave questions that affect mankind as a whole; thus, as already stated, the real interests of mankind have been lost sight of; and each individual, bent on the insane effort to accomplish the impossible, is only adding to the momentum which must finally rupture the bubble we call civilization.   Such is the general effect of the artificial limit to the volume of money!

---

*"What is Property?" by P. J. Proudhon.

46 As elsewhere stated in this book, exchange is as necessary as production; for no one produces everything he needs, and is therefore dependent on others, with whom he must exchange his services, or part or all of his products, for such things as he needs and does not produce. Now, for obvious reasons, we cannot exchange our services or our surplus products direct with those who have for exchange such things as we need. Except in rare instances they do not want what we have to exchange, and when we find one who does, it is almost invariably the case that he has not the articles we need. It follows, therefore, that we have to exchange indirectly instead of directly, and hence the necessity for a medium of exchange—a universal order for goods—that, delivering your product or services, you get an order for an equal amount of products, good anywhere where they are offered for sale. Such is a medium of exchange called money (4, 10); and it is those who incur the risk when they part with their services or property who should decide on what conditions it shall be furnished; because, as elsewhere explained, it is a worthless thing in itself (301), of no market value, and only possessing a purchasing power equal to its face value when honestly issued. And the more one examines into the merits of the case, the more he is convinced that this view is the correct one; but instead of this being the case, we find that it is a class that has little or no direct interest in exchange of products, that decides not only on what conditions it shall be furnished, but they also determine how much shall be furnished, and do all in their power to prevent those interested from supplying themselves. Think of a class of individuals who have no direct interest in transportation, hav-

ing the exclusive control over the supply of locomotives, and deciding that so many per 100,000 of the population is amply sufficient to do the hauling. "What nonsense!" the reader will exclaim. But is it not equally as absurd to allow a class to control the means of exchange as it would be to allow a set of men to control the means of transportation? The power over the destinies of men is more effectual through the control of money than of anything else, and that is precisely why the ruling class use this means. This control must be brought to an end; for there is not the slightest excuse for it, and there is every reason why those engaged in production and exchange should assume it themselves.

47 To make this matter still clearer it is not necessary to present proof, for all who have had any experience in business know, to their sorrow, that among the number who obtain goods on credit, there are some who fail to pay. In this kind of credit (unsecured credit)(9), then, there is a certain loss from bad debts. There is also the inconvenience of having to part with the goods without receiving the money for them until some time in the future. Now, the Mutual Credit System proposes to put an end to these two evils by doing away entirely with unsecured credit, substituting secured credit (paper money)(12). Instead of an individual obtaining credit in products of those who sell, he obtains certificates of credit of the Mutual Credit Association, for which he furnishes ample security; thus only those who have security can obtain credit in the form of certificates of credit (60). That puts an end to bad debts—one of the two evils just mentioned.

48 By the use of these certificates, which constitute the best money that can be devised, all business transactions can be conducted on a cash basis; thus putting an end to the other evil—the inconvenience resulting from the delay in collecting for the goods sold. Independent of other benefits that would follow, we have, then, in the Mutual Credit System, the means of inaugurating universal cash payments;

the cash — certificates of credit — being amply secured.
What better argument can be presented in favor of the new
system than the proposition to gradually convert all book
accounts into ready cash?

49   In granting credit as it is now done, business men
rely mainly on the reports of firms who make a specialty of
inquiring into the business standing of individuals; so that
whether or not one can obtain the credit he asks, depends
very largely upon these reports.   If he is given the credit, it
means that he obtains goods without paying for them immediately, and that those who give the credit are minus the
amount of the credit until the goods are paid for.   Under
this absurd system, it is not the party who *gets* the benefit of
the credit, but the party who *confers* the benefit who takes
all the risk.   The New Philosophy of Money teaches that
the party who desires credit, instead of asking others to take
the risk involved in giving him credit, he should assume that
risk himself, and proposes the Mutual Credit System as the
means of attaining that end.

50   It so happens that it is inherent in the very nature of
economics, that that which is the most advantageous to the
community as a whole, at the same time invariably presents
an irresistable attraction.   Man is still moved by his cupidity.
It is to this propensity, mainly, that we are indebted for the
advantages we now enjoy, and it is upon it that we must
depend for those that are yet to come.   The Mutual Credit
System of money is not lacking in its irresistable attraction
— its vital force, that which will outweigh all obstacles and
defeat all opposition — its appeal to man's cupidity.   The
borrower, like the purchaser, is interested in himself.   He
will not long pay high rates of interest when he knows how
to supply himself at low rates; just the same as a purchaser
will not pay one merchant a higher price for goods than he
can buy them for elsewhere.

51   We have seen, then, that the reasons why business
men and not money-lenders should provide the medium of

exchange, and have entire control of it, are overwhelming; and we have seen that the inducement is altogether too great for this class to resist the temptation. When they take a hand in investigating and realize that they can save from 5 to 10 per cent on the money they borrow, it can be safely stated that they will do it.

52 We apply the term "scarce" to things that are natural products or those produced by nature, and also to artificial products or such things as are produced by labor or devised by the ingenuity of man; but we do not reason the same with reference to the scarcity of the one as of the other. When we say that diamonds are scarce, we state a fact about which there is no use in reasoning any further, as we could not possibly increase the quantity. Not so with regard to the artificial products. If there is a scarcity relative to the demand for any of these artificial products, ingenuity at once sets to work to devise means of increasing the supply. This is true of every artificial thing except money, although money is essentially artificial. Why this exception? We hear it stated, and we know from experience that it is true, that money is scarce. If it were any other article than money there would be no end to the efforts made to increase the supply. If money is of artificial origin, why can we not increase its supply just as we do any other artificial thing? Naturally, or in reality, money is not an exception; and the effect of supply and demand would be as effectual in regulating the quality and quantity of money as it has been in producing sound and cheap insurance, ease and comfort in travel, the printing press, or any and all the advantages of applied science and art. If by a certain procedure a printed bill can be converted into a "dollar," made to circulate as money, cancel indebtedness and be acceptable in exchange for commodities, why cannot this method be extended until we satisfy all demands for money, and make it possible to do all business on a cash basis, instead of the enforced unsecured credit system of today? Why must a

"civilized" community be startled every few weeks by a
gigantic, unexpected and unnecessary failure, and every
day by numerous smaller ones?   Why must the individual's
business success be a game of chance in which he may slave
during the vigorous part of his life and be left penniless in
his old age?   Why is our system of credit so destitute of
scientific method?   It is pure guesswork, and is doubly
damnable in that it offers a premium to rascality and defeats
honesty.   Is not the question of granting credit, either at a
bank, financially, or by a merchant, commercially, a matter
of guesswork?   How can one know that the individual
seeking credit will be able to meet his obligations?

53   In financial circles, where there is less competition
and monopoly is more concentrated, an endorser is demanded;
but who is the endorser?   He may be a friend of the borrower who knows little of how his balance sheet would figure, but considers him an honest man, and yet he may be
deceived.   He may be a patron of the bank whom it considers good, and who, on account of his extensive transactions
and his prominence in society, it is reluctant to refuse.   Here
we have favoritism and uncertainty.   Or, again, both
endorser and endorsee may be engaged in "kiting" to save
themselves from the effects of previous schemes of which
they had, perhaps, been victims.   The scarcity of money
and the consequent monopoly of credit produce these results,
and induce otherwise honest and fair-minded citizens to resort
to deceit and false pretense to "bridge over" and save themselves and dependent ones from poverty, which the system
and not themselves individually, is responsible for.   What
should we think of a system that offers greater inducements
to play false than to be truthful and honest?

54   If the present system is so defective, so inconsistent
with the spirit of progress and so conducive to immorality
and injustice in its effects, are these not sufficient reasons
why we should investigate any new system which claims it
will afford relief?

55   The supply of a sufficient volume of perfectly reliable medium of exchange to enable all commercial transactions to be cash—secured credit instead of unsecured credit—is not only essential to prosperity, justice and morality, but is as simple and easy of accomplishment as to establish and conduct building and loan associations or insurance companies. It is, in fact, so irrational to have a scarcity of money, that it will be hard to make the next generation believe such was the case (77).

56   If it is not scarcity of money (secured credit) that compels a resort to book or time credits (unsecured credit), what is it that does?   If accounts are finally to be settled by the payment of money—the transfer of secured credit —why defer it thirty, sixty, ninety days, or six months? If there is not enough money to cancel indebtedness, how can postponement of settlement make it any more possible of accomplishment?   If a dollar will not pay a debt of two dollars, much less ten or twenty, now, will it in thirty, sixty, ninety days, or six months, or ever? (75-77).

57   Debt in the form of unsecured credit, book accounts, promises to pay, etc., is not transferable in exchange for commodities as secured credit in the form of paper money is. Why, then, do we go on contracting obligations in the form we know to a certainty we cannot meet, when we could just as well contract them in a form we know with equal certainty we could meet?   It is true that not all unsecured credits could be converted into secured credits; not all who have an account current with one or more merchants could put up security to borrow certificates of credit of the Mutual Credit Association; but it is equally true that if those who could put up security were offered the opportunity to do so, and get certificates of credit at 1 per cent per annum, with which they could buy at cash prices, there would soon be enough in circulation to enable all transactions to be conducted on a cash basis.*   It is not necessary that everybody should bor-

*See foot note, page 19.

row money in order that there be plenty in circulation. Those who have wealth will always use it to the best advantage to themselves that they know of. If, under a correct system of money, interest is abolished, and, as a necessary result, dividends also, as they are but a form of interest, capitalists will still be anxious to employ their wealth, if only for the purpose of preserving it; as wealth not in use decays more rapidly than when in use, and the enterprise that uses the wealth as capital will naturally have to sustain the loss from wear and tear and decay. The capitalist will therefore seek every opportunity for investment, availing himself of the advantage which the Mutual Credit Association affords of credit in that most desirable form—paper money.*

58 Thus it can be readily seen that the incentive to borrow money when the rate is only 1 per cent per annum, or less, in order to get the benefit of cash prices, will be very great, and all will avail themselves of the opportunity who can. Hence there will always be all the money in circulation necessary to do an entirely cash business.

----

*Credit, the great lever in human progress, will then be worked at long range and "for all it is worth." It will not work disastrously as it does now, because it will be secured instead of unsecured credit. It will be live credit, in the available form of a medium of exchange, instead of dead credit in the unavailable form of book accounts.

59   Where the system of money is such that the supply is furnished direct from the printing press to borrowers who can put up security, as The New Philosophy of Money teaches is the proper way, there cannot be too much or too little money (35).

60   It is for the individual who can put up security to decide whether he needs money or not—no one else can decide it for him—and it is the business of the institutions that supply it, to furnish him, on application, the sum he is entitled to in proportion to the security he is prepared to pledge (47).   What applies to one individual applies to all.

61   If, then, all borrowers who can comply with the rules as to security, are accommodated with money; if the rules do not discriminate in favor of certain securities and against others, as is the case now (19-21); if everything that has a market value can be used as a basis for credit in the form of paper money, how could there be too little money?

62   The same reasoning applies to the opposite—too much. If only such as could comply with the rules are furnished money, how could there be too much?

63   It is truly difficult in some instances to show up an absurdity. In this case, the difficulty consists in the fact that the parties who talk about too much money, have really nothing definite in their minds when they make the statement. Unless you know what an opponent means, how can you discuss it? And if he does not know himself, how can anyone else? The only way to do is to take the statement for what it is worth. "Too much money!" The bare statement is as meaningless as blows struck with a cane on the sidewalk. If it is stated of a depreciated paper money, then

there must be a supplemental statement, expressing in proportion to what is there too much money. It is not the volume of money in itself that affects its purchasing power, but the proportion of volume to security. Whatever holds good with regard to one paper dollar, applies with equal force to any number of paper dollars. To illustrate: The amount of security that will sustain one paper dollar in circulation at its face value, multiplied any number of times will sustain that number of paper dollars in circulation at their face value. If additional paper money is issued without additional security, the purchasing power of that paper money will be reduced in proportion; but if an additional amount is issued, with additional security in the same proportion, the addition to the volume of paper money will not affect its purchasing power, provided the security is ready at any time, or at any definite stated time not too remote, to redeem it; and provided the facts are well known and there are no parties who are deceiving the public in regard to them.

64 The trouble with those who honestly maintain the opinion that the Mutual Credit System would result in too much money, is that they apply to this system the reasoning that applies to the specie basis system. In that system specie is the basis of the issue, that is, paper money is issued in place of coin; and it follows that the more paper money issued in proportion to the coin it is issued on, the less basis, and the less the chances of getting the coin when it is demanded. One dollar in coin cannot redeem more than one dollar in paper, and when there are two dollars in paper to one in coin, it is inflation. The more paper money issued in excess of the security it is issued on, the more inflation and the less its purchasing power, is perfectly correct; but the theory has prevailed so long and is so universal, that paper money must be redeemable in coin, and as coin is an exceedingly scarce commodity, the idea of plenty of paper money has become associated with that which is impossible. Such reasoning, however, is with-

3

out foundation, and results from the failure to correctly understand the Mutual Credit System.   In the specie basis system,
as we have seen, there is no escape from either one of two
evils; a volume of money limited to the quantity of coin or
inflation; but under the Mutual Credit System there can
be plenty of money without inflation.

65   The argument that "when gold is used as money
there is no doubt about its value (200), as there is about
paper money," applies to gold only, not to paper money
issued on gold; but as we cannot dispense with paper
money and confine ourselves to the use of gold only,
the argument is of no weight, and the question at issue nar-
rows itself down to this: Since paper money is not wealth,
but a representative of wealth; since it is not value, but
credit; and since we cannot use wealth, but must use the
representative; since we cannot use value in exchange, but
must resort to credit; how can we devise a system that will
supply credit in the form of paper money, which will contain the least possible element of uncertainty?   And it is in
answer to this question that the Mutual Credit System
appeals to our judgment (6).

66 Under this title, the Century Company, of New York, published, in 1892, a pamphlet, a reprint from the "Century Magazine," giving an account of "cheap money experiments in past and present times." Chapter I, entitled "The People and Finance," says: "There are a few elementary principles in economic science, the mastery of which by the great body of the American people would be of incalculable value to us as a nation. One of these is that no government can create money out of anything which it may choose to call money. Another is that all classes of the people, rich and poor, laborer and employer, are far better off with a sound and stable currency than they are with any of the varieties of 'cheap money'."

67 The great difficulty that besets an effort to get a clear comprehension of economic questions is the misunderstanding in the use of terms. The question arises, what, in reality, constitutes a sound and stable currency, and what cheap money? What does the writer of the statement just quoted mean by these terms, and what do these terms signify in the minds of those who claim that money can be cheap and that there can be plenty of it? There is evidence all through the pamphlet that by "a sound and stable currency" is meant gold, or paper money that is convertible into gold at its face value. It is also quite apparent that by the term "cheap money" is meant money that is not sound and stable; and by quoting the term it is intended to attribute to money reformers (those who claim that money can be plenty and cheap) a desire to have or put into circulation money that is not sound and stable. Now, is it reasonable to suppose that there are people who deliberately prefer a depreci-

ated paper money, or one that is liable to depreciate, to one
that is not liable to depreciation?   The system advocated by
any particular set of money reformers may be a fallacy, and
result, if put in operation, in a depreciated paper money; but
to imply that such is the end they desire to attain; to attribute to them the deliberate intention of trying to establish a
system of money that is not sound and stable, is a perversion
of fact, and the one who states it is an unfair disputant.
Why have we not as much right to accuse him of deliberately defending a system that was devised and established in
the interest of money-lenders and to the great detriment of
everybody else?   It is not true that money reformers prefer
to have depreciated money, nor is that the end they are striving for.   It is not true that we cannot have such an abundance of money that no one will say "money is scarce," as
they do now, without it becoming depreciated.   When a
money reformer speaks of the need for cheap money, he
does not mean what this writer does when he speaks of
"cheap money."   The former means a low rate of interest,
which is the price we pay for money; using the term *cheap* in
the same sense that we do when we say, "potatoes are very
cheap this year," or "strawberries are cheap at this season of
the year."   The quality is not referred to at all.   But this
writer does not refer to the rate of interest when he says
cheap money.   He means a depreciated paper money, and he
cites many of the most wild and delusive schemes that have
come and gone, to prove that cheap money is a delusion.
The following from the last chapter emphatically declares it
to be such: "We began with a plain exposition of the imperative need on the part of the people of this country of a
clear conviction that no money except the best was worth
the having, and that 'cheap money' in any and all forms is a
delusion from which all people should pray to be delivered."
Applying to the term cheap money the definition which he
does, namely: depreciated money or money which must
inevitably depreciate, everybody must necessarily agree with

him; but applying the meaning which money reformers have
in mind when they use the term, namely: money, the interest
or price of which is low, who will agree with him?   Only
money-lenders, large capitalists and those who are too ignorant to know any better.   It is an unfair, not to say dishonest perversion of fact.   Continuing, this "Cheap Money Ret-
rospect" says: "From this we passed to a historical survey
of the more notable of the many experiments which have
been made in various countries and times to improve the
condition of states and nations by making money cheap and
plentiful."

68   It is not difficult to detect the animus that prompted
this effort in the interest of money-lenders, but if evidence is
needed, we have not far to go for it.   On the 45th page of
this pamphlet, the writer says in reference to the failure to
establish the English Land Bank in 1696:   "The capitalists
would not put their money into it because its avowed object
was to injure them by lowering the rate of interest and les-
sening the demand for existing money" (19-21).

69   Here we have an admission that capitalists are opposed
to and exert their influence to prevent an increase in the volume of money, because a scarcity of money keeps up the rate
of interest; and that the failure to establish this bank was
due to their opposition.

70   This admission gives away his case, for he points out
no natural obstacle in the way of plenty of money and low
rates of interest, but presents numerous unwise and impracticable schemes that have failed, to prove the impossibility of
its attainment, while he inadvertantly admits that it is really
the opposition of the money power that has prevented it.
How empirical is this attempt at instruction can be appreci-
ated when it is realized that the money power rules in consequence of the ignorance and superstition of the masses; when
it is fully comprehended, as set forth in The New Philosophy of Money, that the money borrower with good security
is not dependent upon the money-lender, except as the law,

made at the dictation and in the interest of the money-lender,
is supposed to make him so.   But not even does the law, nor
can it make him dependent, and the realization of cheap
money and plenty of it, is only a question of enlightenment
and freedom from superstition.

71   There are a few elementary principles in economic
science, the mastery of which by the "great financiers," professors and those who presume to instruct the people through
the magazines and the press generally, would be of incalculable value to us all, individually and collectively.   One of
these is that this government has not and never had any
authority to impose a tax on the issue of paper money unless
it is imposed on all issues alike; it has no constitutional right
to discriminate in favor of any particular issue.   Another is
that the Mutual Credit System will furnish plenty of cheap
money that the money power will not be able to depreciate.
They are playing fast and loose with the most serious and
vital question we are confronted with; saying to the people
who know little or nothing of the subject: "abandon all hope
of plenty of money or low rates of interest"; and in order to
induce them to believe it and resign themselves to the hard-
ships the present money system imposes, they are treated to
a rehash of all the stupid schemes that speculators, money
sharks and political tyrants have been able to foist upon
the people, as though these contained the least particle of
evidence that cheap money and plenty of it is not a possibility.

72　According to the United States Treasury Report for the month of March, 1894, the volume of money in circulation was $24.85 per capita. The method pursued in order to obtain this data, is as follows: From the total amount of coin money minted, and paper money printed and issued is deducted, as near as can be ascertained, the amount lost or destroyed; the coin money consumed in the arts and manufactures, and the difference between the amount imported and exported, and also the amount of paper money withdrawn from circulation is taken into account. From the amount thus arrived at, called the "general stock," is deducted the amount in the treasury. The balance is said to be in circulation.

73　The phrase "in circulation" is misleading. It conveys the idea that the amount to which it refers is actually circulating—being exchanged for commodities and services—whereas a proportion of it (no one can tell how much), is hoarded; there is constantly a large amount lying idle in safe deposit vaults and in banks; the amount destroyed and the excess exported compared with the amount returned cannot be even approximately estimated, and not all the jewelers and manufacturers who employ the "precious" metals report the amount of coin they consume; so that this data is largely guesswork. But suppose it were accurate and reliable. Let it be admitted that there is twice, or even four times that much money "in circulation." What of it? Of what advantage is it to borrowers who have security that is acceptable to money-lenders, but who cannot afford to pay the rate of interest they charge, to know that these money-lenders have

plenty of money to loan?   Of what good is it to the people
whose security is rejected by the money-lenders, to know
that they have plenty of money to loan?   The financial jour-
nals and the press of the country generally, mock at the distress of the people when they say "there is plenty of money
in the country."   It is as reasonable as it would be to tell
people who are suffering from a scarcity of ice in midsum-
mer, that there is plenty of ice at the north pole; or to the
traveler in the desert of Sahara who is perishing with thirst,
that there is plenty of cool water a thousand feet beneath
him.   Of what use is it that "there is plenty of money
in the country," if those who need it cannot get it?   For
whom is there "plenty of money?"   For the money-lenders?   There is always too much for them.

74   If money is a tool, why reason in regard to it differ-
ently from the way we reason with regard to any other tool?
How strange it would appear to our judgment if the claim
were put forward that there are too many vessels to drink
out of; that the number should be limited to so many per
capita, whereas there are many times that number; that the
quantity manufactured should be restricted so that there
never could be more than so many for each individual of the
entire population at any given time.   "How stupid!" most
people will exclaim.   "It would be very inconvenient to try
to get along with a tenth or a twentieth of the number of
cups, glasses, mugs, etc., and the inconvenience would be a
far greater evil than the cost of these articles; besides if only
a few could make such things, or if there were only so
many made prices would go up, the rich would buy all they
wanted and the poor could not get any!"   But to limit the
volume of money (19-21) to so many dollars per capita,
which most people are reconciled to, is equally as stupid.
Suppose all the money in the whole country were offered to
borrowers who had good security, at one per cent per annum.
How long would it take to exhaust the whole pile?   And
what would the rest of the borrowers do who came after all

the money had been loaned out? If there is enough security in the country free from incumbrance, the money would all be borrowed in less than a week. If this is correct, then the rate of interest determines very largely the amount of money that will circulate. If interest is very high, large amounts of money will lie idle in the banks.* If interest is low enough, all the money will be borrowed that can be furnished (35, 60) until all labor is employed and all enterprising individuals are fully engaged, and therefore (if that time should ever come) no additional money will be needed.

75 What, then, has the number of individuals in a country to do with the volume of money? It is claimed now that there is plenty of money. According to Mr. Bennett's estimate (118-126) the wealth in the United States amounts to $72,000,000,000; and according to the United States Treasurer's Report for April, 1894, the total amount of paper money representing that wealth was $1,081,499,270, or a proportion of about one dollar credit in the form of paper money for every sixty-six dollars worth of wealth. Is it any wonder these manipulators of the currency would rather give the volume of money per capita—$24.85 per head—than $1.00 per every $66.00 of the wealth. Mr. Bennett also shows (121) that the interest charge on the active capital of the country is $3,300,000,000. It follows, therefore, that if all this interest were paid in paper money, all there is in the country, which is not one-third the amount of this interest charge, would have to pass into the hands of the capitalists three times during the year and then there would still be a trifle over $50,000,000 unpaid.

76 Overwhelmingly crushing as this evidence is of the imbecility or knavery (which?) of those who control the currency, and of the utter stupidity of the per capita idea of

*To those who control money, the incentive to keep up the rate of interest is that if there is great demand they get high rates on all they have to loan. If they only loan half what they have at 10 per cent it is equal to 5 per cent on the whole; whereas if they loan two-thirds at 6 per cent it would be only 4 per cent on the whole.

the volume of money needed, their confusion can be still worse confounded by additional evidence.   Mr. Bennett says (122): "At the very lowest estimate, $897,000,000 must be charged yearly to government in the United States, not including the payment of the principal of the public debt. This representing money spent outside of regular business . . . . Is it any wonder that we have financial panics when the volume of money is so contracted, compared with the enormous duty it has to perform?"

77   So, not only does all this money have to pass three times during the year into the possession of the capitalists in payment for the use of their capital, but more than four-fifths of it must also pass, during the same period, into the hands of government officials to satisfy all the various demands it makes upon us.   And all this in addition to its function in the exchange of commodities, which is beyond power to estimate.   Of course the answer to this argument to show the necessity for more money, which the conservatives and the superficial will make, will be the statement that checks, drafts or bills of exchange, etc., are so extensively used that about nine-tenths of all exchanges are settled by means of them and only about one-tenth by the use of money.   But since, to get a draft or use a check one must first have the money, their use does not affect the argument in the least, and the fact remains that the demands for money cannot possibly be met with the volume of money available; and while there is no way of determining how much money is really necessary to perform conveniently such an enormous aggregate of payments, it is probable that twenty times what we now have will be in constant circulation under the Mutual Credit System.

78 "If there exists an agency of unquestioned power, it surely is that of credit. Who does not admire its wonderful potency? Who does not recognize the mighty share which is due to it in the economic development of the present age?"*—*Cyclopædia of Political Science.*

79 In discussing a vast and complicated question, such as economics, it is indispensable that the matter of terminology should be well understood and mutually agreed upon by all parties to the discussion. The definitions for the term credit the writer has thus far met with, seem inadequate, and he has ventured to formulate such as will more clearly define it as applied in The New Philosophy of Money, and hopes there will be no cause for rejecting them.

80 The term credit designates all transactions that are not barter, or settlement on the spot by the exchange of equivalents in value, or that which is accepted as such.

81 Coin money being value and accepted as such in exchange for commodities, transactions with coin money are not credit transactions, but must be defined as barter.

82 Credit is divided into two kinds or forms. One is secured credit, the other is unsecured credit (9).

83 Paper money is a form of credit, and *should be secured credit.*

84 An appropriate definition for secured credit would seem to be: debt incurred with ample provision made to insure payment.

85 A promissory note secured by a pledge of collateral, such as a mortgage note, etc., is secured credit.

---

*If the above can be said of credit generally, it can much more emphatically be said of that form of credit furnished by the Mutual Credit System—secured credit (83).

86 A simple unsecured promissory note is unsecured
credit. Book accounts are generally unsecured credits. It
might be argued that coin is accepted as money and not as
value; that, with the exception of a few manufacturers who
melt it up to consume it, people do not use it otherwise than
they do paper money. Very true; *but it is taken because it
has value.* It would not be taken if it had none. If the
government were to reduce the gold and silver in its coins to
one-half what they contain now, their purchasing power
would decline one-half,—while credit money is taken because
it is believed that it is ultimately to be taken up out of circulation by giving for it what its face calls for in market value.
The distinguishing feature between the two kinds of money
—credit money and commodity money—is the fact that the
former is what the adjective credit signifies,—an obligation
to pay which some one has contracted to meet, and has
pledged enough value to guarantee those who take it, that it
will be met and paid at maturity. This is what they rely
on, and not, as in the case of coin money, on the market
value of the material of which it is made.

87 This latter money, on the other hand, is not credit.
There is no obligation or agreement whatever, on the part
of anyone. It is recognized by what it states on its face, as
to what it is, and it is accepted as such. There is no promise
on the part of anyone, as in the case of credit money, that it
will be taken in exchange for anything else at any specified
time.

88 It would appear that enough has been said to demonstrate that paper money is credit money, and that, therefore,
the exchange of commodities for paper money is a credit
transaction; and that coin money being wealth—market
value—there being nothing in the nature of credit about it,
and that those who take it rely entirely upon the market
value it contains that they will be able to exchange it at its
face value for other commodities, and that if it fails they
have no recourse but to suffer the loss, it must be defined as

commodity money; and that the exchange of commodity money for commodities is in the nature of, and must therefore be defined as barter (65).

89 It will hardly be necessary to present argument to show that there are two forms of credit—secured and unsecured—or that it is correct and desirable as well as convenient to thus classify them (9).

90 Probably no one will object to the statement that credit in the form of paper money should be secured credit; or to the classification made with reference to secured and unsecured credit. Certainly unsecured notes and book accounts as they are generally conducted, or when no provision is made to insure payment, are unsecured credit.

91 As to the definition for secured credit—debt incurred with ample provision made to insure payment—the writer would be glad to have anyone suggest a better.

92 We now come to a point in the discussion of this question of credit where the enormous advantages of the Mutual Credit System can be still further indisputably demonstrated.

93 It will be granted, of course, that secured credit is better than unsecured credit; that paper money that circulates at its face value in payment of debt and in exchange for commodities is better than book accounts or promissory notes. It is more useful and therefore more desirable. This proposition, it would seem, is too apparent to require argument. Since the actual cost of paper money is insignificant, much less than bookkeeping the same amounts, why is it that credit does not take that form? Why is it that credit almost universally takes the unsecured form, although it is the least desirable, the most inconvenient and the most costly? It is not easy to explain many of the strange phenomena connected with man and his methods, but it is not difficult to realize that when he follows the most inconvenient of the various ways open to him, it must be because he is ignorant.

94 We do not see people walking up six or ten flights of

stairs in preference to taking the elevator, or go long distances to talk with some one when they could just as well "hello" to him by means of the telephone. They are not in the habit of hiring wagons in preference to traveling on railroads, nor do they go walking (intentionally) where the mud or snow is deepest. Why, then, do they not follow this propensity to save labor and avoid inconveniences in the matter of exchange as well as getting up-stairs, talking to one another at a distance, or a thousand other things that are done in the most convenient and least laborious way that is known? There can be only one answer to this question. It is the logic, as well as the fact that they are ignorant. The means are at their command at any time to put an end to unsecured credit by establishing Mutual Credit Associations to furnish certificates of credit,—paper money *secured*. This *secured* credit being cheaper, vastly more convenient and far safer, would gradually take the place of book credit, promissory notes and other forms of unsecured credit. If it has not been done, it is because of the general prevailing ignorance on this subject.

95 In "Mutual Banking," page 50, I find the following: "All the questions connected with credit, the usury laws, etc., may be forever set at rest by the establishment of MUTUAL BANKS. Whoever goes to the Mutual Bank and offers real property in pledge, may always obtain money: for the Mutual Bank can issue money to any extent; and that money will always be good, since it is all of it based on actual property that may be sold under the hammer. The interest will always be at a less rate than one per cent per annum, since it covers, not the insurance of the money loaned, there being no such insurance required, as the risk is 0; since it covers, not the damage which is done the bank by keeping it out of its money, as that damage is also 0, the bank having always an unlimited supply remaining on hand, so long as it has a printing press and paper; since it covers, plainly and simply, the mere expenses of the institution,—clerk hire, rent, printing, paper, etc. And it is fair that such expenses should be paid under the form of a rate of interest; for thus each one contributes to bear the expenses of the bank, and in

the precise proportion of the benefits he individually experiences from it. Thus, the interest, properly so called, is 0: and we venture to predict that the Mutual Bank will one day give all the real credit that will be given; for since this bank will give such at 0 per cent interest per annum, it will be difficult for other institutions to compete with it for any length of time. The day is coming when everything that is bought will be paid for on the spot, and in mutual money; when all payments will be made, all wages settled on the spot. The Mutual Bank will never, of course, give personal credit; for it can issue bills only on wealth. It cannot enter into partnership with anybody; for, if it issues bills where there is no real guaranty furnished for their repayment, it vitiates the currency and renders itself unstable. Personal credit will one day be given by individuals, only; that is, capitalists will one day enter into PARTNERSHIP with enterprising and capable men who are without capital, and the profits will be divided between the parties according as their contract of partnership may run. Whoever, in the times of the Mutual Bank, has property, will have money, also; and the laborer who has no property will find it very easy to get it; for every capitalist will seek to secure him as a partner. All services will then be paid for in ready money and the demand for labor will be increased three, four and five fold.

95a "As for credit of the kind that is idolized by the present generation, credit which organizes society on feudal principles, confused credit, the Mutual Bank will obliterate it from the face of the earth. Money furnished under the existing system, to individuals and corporations is principally applied to speculative purposes, advantageous, perhaps, to those individuals and corporations, if the speculations answer; but generally disadvantageous to the community, whether they answer or whether they fail. If they answer, they generally end in a monopoly of trade, great or small, and in consequent high prices; if they fail, the loss falls on the community. Under the existing system there is little safety for the merchant. The utmost degree of caution practicable in business has never yet enabled a company or individual to proceed for any long time without incurring bad debts.

95b "The existing organization of credit is the daughter of hard money, begotten upon it incestuously by that insufficiency of circulating medium which results from laws making specie the sole legal tender. The immediate consequences of confused credit are want of confidence, loss of time, commercial frauds, fruitless and repeated applications for payment, complicated with irregular and ruinous expenses. The ultimate consequences are bad debts, expensive accommodation loans, law suits, insolvency, bankruptcy, separation of classes, hostility, hunger, extravagance, distress, riots, civil war, and, finally, revolution. The natural consequences of mutual banking are, first of all, the creation of order and the definitive establishment of due organization in the social body; and ultimately the cure of all the evils which flow from the present incoherence and disruption in the relations of production and commerce."

96   Ruskin says: "Value is the life-giving power of anything; cost, the quantity of labor required to produce it; price, the quantity of labor which its possessor will take in exchange for it."

97   Josiah Warren, in his "True Civilization" (a work which, unfortunately, is out of print), laid down the principle that *cost should be the limit of price.* He did not mean that there should be a law prohibiting people from charging more than cost, but that long experience as a merchant and profound study on the subject had brought him to the conclusion that that statement embodied a principle that perfect freedom in production and exchange would demonstrate to be correct, because it would be the result that we should attain when all legislative interference ceased. Ruskin says: "Cost is the quantity of labor required to produce anything." These writers agree, and their view of it is in harmony with The New Philosophy of Money. The Mutual Credit System furnishes certificates of credit at cost (95). Cost, of course, includes every item of expense; from the material, which is concrete labor, to the finished product delivered to the consumer. Cost, therefore, should be the quantity of labor required to produce, or an equivalent of the amount required to compensate all labor expended in production. This should be the limit of price, because if price exceeds this limit, it must include a bonus to some one. But who is entitled to something for which he does not render an equivalent? Under the Mutual Credit system, alone, can mutualism or co-operation be successful. Without it, capitalists can checkmate any effort in that direction that they choose; but the Mutual Credit System can be inaugurated without their aid and in spite of their opposition. When co-operation becomes general, cost will be the limit of price.

4

98 What nobody wants has no value. Per contra: that which people want, providing it costs labor to produce it, has value; the proportion in a given object depending upon the number of people who want it, and the ease or difficulty with which it can be obtained. This is market or exchangable value. The value of an object, and, therefore, the relative value of all objects, is expressed by means of the abstraction which in this country is called "dollar"; more or less value being expressed by one or any multiple or fraction thereof. Thus we say $1.01,—one dollar and one cent—or one dollar and the one-hundredth part of one dollar; the two last figures running from 1 to 99 and expressing that many hundredths of a dollar. This conventional term, whatever it may be in any country, is always also the monetary unit, and what should be but seldom is, secured credit, in the form of paper money, or value (wealth) in the form of commodity money (coin) is divided up to correspond with the value expressed by this conventional term, thus facilitating its transfer in exchange for commodities in amounts corresponding with the exact value of the commodities to be exchanged, or the exact amount of debt to be paid.

99 There is another kind of value, by which is meant utility. The portrait of a relative or dear friend has a utility for those whose friend he or she was; its possession affords pleasure. It may or may not have a market value. The air has no market value, but it has a utility value—we could not live without it. If a method could be discovered by which it could be bottled up or pumped into tanks, no doubt Congress would grant special privileges to a few to deprive the rest of it, like it has done with the land, and sell it to them at

a high price. It would then have a market value. That which adds to our comfort, affords enjoyment, in short, whatever satisfies want, has utility value. But not all things which have utility value have market or exchangable value. Market value represents labor, or monopoly and labor. If there were no monopoly, nothing would be exchangable but labor, either in the form of service or in that concrete form we call commodities.

COMPETITION.

100   "Competition," says the "Twentieth Century,"* "is but a civilized mode of warfare."   The "Century Dictionary" defines it as: "1. The act of seeking or endeavoring to gain what another is endeavoring to gain at the same time; common contest or striving for the same object; rivalry; as the *competition* of two candidates for an office.   2. A trial of skill proposed as a test of superiority or comparative fitness." The "Twentieth Century" continues:

101   "It is not less cruel than the former method of shooting or slashing one's opponent.   Success in either case means the ruin and often the death of the weaker party.   The more humane, the one who shrinks from needless slaughter, often pays for his humanity with crushing defeat.   If we are to continue the competitive system we must be merciless and cold blooded in our competition as on our battlefields.   If we shrink from the necessary consequences of such policy let us .strive for the Co-operative Commonwealth.   It is the only alternative.   Commercial warfare counts more victims yearly than the clash of armies.   The roll of suicides, murders, thefts, defalcations, embezzlements, forgeries, bankruptcies and starvations chargeable to the competitive system in 1893 is a greater aggregate of disasters than is recorded of any war of conquest."

102   The "Twentieth Century" is mistaken.   In the first place, the present system of production and exchange cannot correctly be called the competitive system.   A competitive system is one in which everything is subject to competition, while the present system is dominated by monopoly, which is the opposite of competition.   The evils of which the "Twentieth Century" complains are the result of the *absence* of competition.   The money power, availing itself of the ignorance of the people, secures legislation which excludes competition in supplying that form of credit called paper

*April 12, 1894.

money. By thus limiting credit (15) and by securing franchises through the power money has acquired in consequence of its having been made artificially scarce (359), the large capitalists defeat the competition they would otherwise be subject to, while the wage-earner remains ever exposed to it.

103   The abolition of interest, an abundant supply of money and the gradual reduction of dividends, will cause a constant rise in wages (compensation for personal services), until finally wages absorb all the net increase in wealth (97). Capitalists will then be sure of a return of the full amount invested, instead of about ninety-seven per cent losing part or all they invest, and only about three per cent realizing large fortunes—the inevitable result of compound interest (126, 130). This certainty about the result of investments of capital will be the effect of the abolition of speculation. Competition, which the Mutual Credit System will force monopoly, of whatever nature, to encounter, by the increase in the volume of capital that will result, will put an end to all speculation; for all the wealth in the country will be actively employed as capital in productive enterprise as long as there are idle men and women who want employment. As production under such conditions will be much more rapid than ever before, it will not be long till there will result a surplus of capital, or wealth available as capital, in excess of the demand. Hence, competition among the capitalists to get employees. This will be the direct cause of the rise in wages already mentioned, to the great relief of wage-earners.   How puerile, then, is this tirade on the part of Socialists and Nationalists against competition!

104   Col. Greene, in his pamphlet, "Mutual Banking," says: "As soon as gold and silver are adopted as the legal tender, they are invested with an altogether new utility.   By means of this new utility whoever monopolizes the gold and silver of any country—and the currency is more easily monopolized than any other commodity—obtains control, henceforth over the business of that country; for no man can pay his debts without the permission of the party who

monopolizes the article of legal tender.   Thus, since the
courts recognize nothing as money in the payment of debts
except the article of legal tender, this party is enabled to levy
a tax on all transactions except such as take place without
the intervention of credit.   [Without the intervention of
money, Col. Greene should have said, and it is probable that
the word "credit" is merely a typographical error.—Author.]

105   "By adopting the precious metals as the legal tender
in the payment of debts, society confers a new value upon
them, which new value is not inherent in the metals themselves.   This new value becomes a marketable commodity.
.   .   .   This ought not to be.   .   .   .   This new social
value is inestimable; it is incommensurable with any other
known value whatever.   This money, instead of retaining
its proper relative position, becomes a superior species of
commodity—superior, not in degree, but in kind.   Thus
money becomes the absolute king and the demigod of commodities.   Hence follow great social and political evils.   .
.   .   .   Society established gold and silver as a circulating
medium, in order that exchanges of commodities might be
facilitated; but society made a mistake in so doing; for, by
this very act, it gave to a certain class of men the power of
saying what exchanges *shall*, and what exchanges *shall not
be facilitated*."

106   It would seem unnecessary to add to this statement.
Whoever has watched the course of events, especially of late,
must know that it is true.   How well he understood the
subject can be readily perceived; yet he wrote it about forty
years ago.   The control of money gives the same power
over production and exchange of all commodities, that the
control of the tools by which any single commodity is made
gives over the manufacture of that particular article.   The
control of money, then, excludes competition to a very great
extent, while it makes interest artificially high by making
money artificially scarce.   Labor, on the other hand, has no
means of avoiding competition.   Men and women must work
or starve, and as new inventions, new discoveries and new
processes facilitate production with less labor, the demand for
labor grows less, while competition among wage-earners
grows greater; for those thrown out of work which is no

longer needed must enter other already overcrowded industries, and thus wages are reduced. Now, anyone can see that if the wage-earners had gradually acquired ownership of the means of production—these new inventions, new discoveries and new processes—the advantages derived from them would be enjoyed by the wage-earners themselves. Instead of reducing wages and the number of workers wanted, it would have increased wages and reduced the hours of toil. And since labor produces all wealth, these labor-saving utilities should belong to those who produced them. Whatever, then, has prevented this, is the cause of the evils complained of, and not competition; for we have seen that on the part of the capitalists, so far as the supply of money (which is secured credit)(S3-S4) is concerned, competition is most effectually avoided. Had the capitalists been subject to as severe competition as wage-earners have, then the system could be called the competitive system; but in that case, the evils herein enumerated, and of which we all realize their enormity, would have entirely disappeared, because the capitalist, as a non-producer and an absorber of wealth, would have disappeared.

107   In Mr. Tucker's "Instead of a Book," page 405, is the following interesting paragraph on this subject: "The supposition that competition means war rests upon old notions and false phrases that have been long current, but are rapidly passing into the limbo of exploded fallacies. Competition means war only when it is in some way restricted, either in scope or intensity,—that is, when it is not perfectly free competition; for then its benefits are won by one class at the expense of another, instead of by all at the expense of nature's forces. When universal and unrestricted, competition means the most perfect peace and the truest co-operation; for then it becomes merely a test of forces resulting in their most advantageous utilization. As soon as the demand for labor begins to exceed the supply, making it an easy matter for everyone to get work at wages equal to his product, it is for the interest of all (including his immediate competitors) that the best man should win; which is another way of say-

ing that, where freedom prevails, competition and co-operation are identical."

108   The Mutual Credit System will destroy the speculative part of interest, reducing it to cost of providing the
paper money.   With the cessation of interest will disappear dividends and rent; profit being also reduced to wages
for superintendence.   This will bring us to the competitive
system.   We are not there yet, and it would be well for the
"Twentieth Century" to revise its philosophy and aid in its
realization, instead of retarding it by leading the weak
minded and superficial into the wilderness of unsound ideas;*
for, in the second place, neither the Co-operative Commonwealth nor any other organized body of producers can possibly get along without competition.   Is there to be no "trial
of skill as a test of superiority?"   Will there be no "competitors for office?"   Will there never be "two or more seeking
or endeavoring or striving for the same object?"   Will the
"Twentieth Century" undertake to maintain that these evils
would have existed just the same had there been no monopoly of that form of credit called paper money? or that they
will exist in spite of the establishment of the Mutual Credit
System, the abolition of interest and an abundant supply of
money?

---

*"Special legislation is a covetous pretense that usually steals
heaven's livery the better to serve the devil.   Its pretenses and devices are many, but its favorite cloak is patriotism, because garbed
therein and posing as "country" it can defy exposure, few being
bold enough to assail anything so sacred as country.   The strong
hold of special legislation on the people, and their blindness to its
ruinous effects, is because special legislation identifies itself with
country, and makes opposition thereto opposition to country.   In
spite, however, of patriotic pretenses, the soul of special legislation is
Greed, that base, heartless, never-satisfied passion that seeks its
gratification regardless or in violation of other's rights or sufferings.
Special legislation never seeks its advantage in merit or honest *competition,* but instead, lays hold of law and makes law its servant to
impose burdens and compel obedience."—*"Special Legislation the
Bane of Agriculture,"* by *Lewis H. Blair*

109 The Bible doctrine of interest or usury is very pronounced. In the eighteenth chapter of Ezekiel it says: "The soul that sinneth, it shall die." And then it goes on to say who are those who shall escape this penalty. "He that hath not given forth upon usury, neither hath taken any increase. . . . He is just, he shall surely live, saith the Lord God." This is a terrible anathema, and it is aimed, not at the body, for all bodies die, but it expressly says the soul shall die. This evidently means annihilation.

110 Other quotations might be made equally as denunciatory of the practice,* but this one condemns the modern church and all who receive increase, whether in the form of interest, rent or profit, which exceeds compensation for service, who take the Bible as their guide in morals. But I merely call attention to the fact to show the inconsistency of people who believe in the divinity of the Bible, yet utterly disregard its teachings and defy its threats. It does not concern us in our investigation. We are interested in its philosophy. How does the question present itself on its merits?

111 History proves that the human conscience in all ages of the world has condemned usury; and if there were any merit in altruistic idealism, it would have shown itself capable of realization on this, the most vital of all social questions. The inequity of interest is not a matter of belief. It is susceptible of mathematical demonstration (118-126). Some very interesting calculations have been made at different times showing its incompatibility with the natural order of things (130). It is not only unjust, but its perpetuity is an

---

*Neh. 5; Deut. 23:19; Ps. 15:5; Exodus 22:25; Eze. 18:8, 13; 22:12; Lev. 25:35-37.

utter impossibility.   An ordinary fortune at compound interest would, in a few generations, exceed the wealth of the
largest city; and in a few more, the wealth of the whole
world.

112   The prevalence of interest in excess of cost and risk,
must be harmful or harmless in its effects upon the social
body.   It must be just or unjust to the individuals who have
to pay it; and these are the items we have to consider in
order to settle the question on its merits.

113   In a previous pamphlet, "The Financial Problem,"
the reader will find a comparison made between the rate of
interest and the increase of wealth; showing that the average
rate of interest is from two to three times the actual rate at
which wealth increases.   Attention was called not only to
this disparity between actual and legal increase, but it was
shown that the speed at which we were approaching the
inevitable collapse was being greatly accelerated by the fact
that interest was collected on fictitious values as well as on
that which is the result of labor.

114   The reader should not fail to note the frightful havoc
that is played with common sense, and the utter disregard for
the natural order and constitution of thing, when land values
and the fictitious value added to stocks and bonds, and which
is designated by the appropriate term "water," are not only
sold, thus getting something for nothing, but are made a
basis for interest.   An individual buys a lot for $500, and
builds a house on it which costs him $1,000.   He claims that
"the property" is now worth $3,000, and fixes the rent
accordingly.   Admitting that his time spent in choosing the
plans and watching the building of the house is worth
$500, we have $2,000 as the total cost.   If he now sells out
for $3,000, what does the extra $1,000 represent?   Nothing!
It is fictitious value.   If, instead of selling for all cash, he
gets $2,000 cash and takes a mortgage for $1,000 on which
he receives interest, it is interest on fictitious value.   The
issue of bonds or stock by corporations without adding an

equivalent in real value to the property, is fictitious value, and
if dividends are paid on it, it is interest on fictitious value.

115 Now, if interest on actual values is only a slick way
of robbing people; if it is contrary to and incompatible with
the natural order of things (121-122); how much more so is
interest on fictitious values? If interest limited to actual values will gain faster than those values can be produced by
labor, and it cannot be successfully disputed, how much more
rapidly will its periodical ruin and desolation overtake us if
to the actual values are added enormous sums of fictitious
values which are to draw interest also?

116 The lack of good sense that is displayed by the people generally in dealing with these questions is something
marvelous; but their acquiescense in the prevailing theory of
interest, as well as their silence on the impossibility of its
continuance on the part of the professors of the "science" of
political economy, and the popular and so-called "great financiers," is beyond comprehension, and can only be accounted
for on the ground of ignorance on the subject. It was
pointed out in "The Financial Problem" that millionaires,
failures and poverty are the natural outcome of interest taking, concluding with the following paragraph:

117 "Let me still further reinforce this idea by stating it
in another way. The present social system may be said to
be strangling itself to death. The annual interest charge
exceeding the net annual increase in labor products; or, in
other words, labor produced more wealth during the year
than is actually consumed and there remains a surplus, but
this surplus is not sufficient to meet the amount of interest
demanded by the capitalists for the use of their capital; hence,
as I have already stated, failures are inseparable from the
system."

118 And now comes Mr. J. W. Bennett, of St. Louis,
who, in the March, 1894, number of the "Arena," in the
most powerful article ever published in a magazine on that
subject, demonstrates in a conclusive and unanswerable manner the truth of the above statement, showing the real mon-

etary condition, not only of this country, but of the entire
civilized world. Mr. Bennett gives an estimate of the total
wealth in the United States, its distribution and the proportion that bears interest. He says:

119 "An odd proposition, but one capable of mathematical demonstration, is that the very foundation principles of
our industrial system lead us to recognize obligations which
we can never pay. A simple, specific statement of what
they are, compels us to admit that they are too large to meet.
The present wealth of the United States may be placed in
round numbers at $72,000,000,000. That fully 80 per cent
of this sum pays interest may be verified by any person who
cares to give the subject thought. If any of the money
invested in business bears interest, all money invested in business must likewise bear interest, otherwise nobody would
assume business risks. But we may arrive at the same conclusion by a process quite different.

120 "Something like 80 per cent of the wealth of the
country is in the hands of about 250,000 persons, or about
one two-hundred-fortieth of the population. This excludes
the wealth of well-to-do farmers and merchants; and it goes
without saying that nine-tenths of this wealth held by the
immensely rich is interest-bearing. Nearly all of it is lent,
or, if not lent out it is invested in some business where interest on the money invested is added to the return or profits of
the undertakers.

121 "The wealth in the hands of farmers and merchants
is paying interest on all that is not used for the personal
wants of themselves and their families; and even many of
the homesteads of the country are paying interest. At least
one-half of such wealth is interest-bearing. An examination
of the mortgage lists of the several states will more than bear
out this estimate. We are, then, paying fixed charges, as the
railroads put it, on about $55,000,000,000 of the country's
wealth. The net rate will average 5 per cent; and taking
into consideration commissions and other charges, 6 per cent
is a low estimate of the gross rate. The interest on $55,000,-
000,000 at 6 per cent is $3,300,000,000 per year. To get the
average interest charges for the last decade, we must take
the average of interest-paying capital, which is about $50,-
000,000,000. We have, then, an average yearly interest of
$3,000,000,000, a sum which more than absorbs the entire

yearly increase of wealth in the United States. During the last decade, the wealth of this country has increased about $22,000,000,000. During the same period the interest charges were $30,000,000,000. Adding but the single item of interest on personal business obligations to the standing debt of the people, the assets of the country's citizens will, in the short period of ten years fall $8,000,000,000 below their liabilities. . . . .

122   "But interest and rent charges are not the only liabilities of the business of the country. The government must be supported; the national debt and the interest thereon must be met; debts, state, municipal and school must be provided for; local government must be maintained. The interest on the public debt of the United States amounts to $40,-410,000 annually. The interest on municipal, county and township debts in the United States is $56,750,000 per year. The expenses of the United States, exclusive of interest and the paying off of the standing indebtedness, are now about $350,000,000 yearly, and the cost of state, county and municipal government is $450,000,000 per year. At the very lowest estimate, $897,000,000 must be charged yearly to government in the United States, not including the payment of the principal of the public debt. This, representing money spent outside of regular business, amounts to $8,970,000,000 in a decade. Adding it to the former sum, the excess of interest on private obligations over the increase of wealth, we have $16,970,000,000 as the sum which the assets of the citizens of the United States fall behind their indebtedness every ten years. In view of such figures as these, it is not difficult to see why we have periods of business depression every ten years and terrible financial panics every twenty years.

123   "The tendency under such conditions is to have all the wealth which is not used to feed and shelter and clothe the race pass into the hands of the money-lender. There is a comparatively trifling exception to the rule. About five per cent of all who start in business leave it with more than they began with, and but a portion of their gains can be charged to interest. The more stable and the largest houses of business, however, realize large returns from interest taking.

124   "What wonder is it, then, that the business of the country has to go periodically into the hands of a receiver, in order to straighten out its accounts and begin anew? This

is the only way in which the great bulk of business men can get a new start. Creditors are obliged to take part of their claims, as there is not enough to pay the whole. Debts are canceled and a new start is made. The wealth is lent out again; interest is paid again until the burden gets too large and another crash comes. At each crash some of the men who were creditors at the last accounting are found among the debtor class, and thus property is prevented from massing in a decade or two in the hands of a permanent creditor caste. Yet the circle is forever growing narrower.

125 "After keeping up the capital stock of the world, and feeding, sheltering and clothing the race, there is not enough left to satisfy the demands of the money-lender. If one agrees to return every ten, twelve, or even twenty years, an amount equal to that which he has borrowed, in interest, he is undertaking an impossibility. Nature has no such productive power. If it cannot be done in this country of virgin resources and unparalleled conditions for the production of wealth, it can be done nowhere. We are, then, confronted by a foundation principle of our financial system which necessarily results in business panic. It is necessary that this principle of our system be critically examined if we would find where our trouble lies. . . . .

126 "If interest taking is right, compound interest taking is right. The principle of compound interest is that a dollar, without any exertion on the owner's part, will grow into two dollars in a given number of years, four dollars in less than twice that time, eight dollars in less than three times the original period, and will keep on increasing in more than geometrical ratio, until that one dollar with its interest would, after a time, represent all of the wealth on earth (130). The rate makes no difference as to the principle of the thing. Money at compound interest will just as truly increase indefinitely at 5 as at 25 per cent, though more slowly, to be sure."

127 But Mr. Bennett's article is replete with fact and sound logic, annihilating the sophistry of the political economists and "great financiers" at every turn.

128 There are two points, however, where Mr. Bennett differs with The New Philosophy of Money. On page 518 he says: "Interest taking is the foundation of speculative

business." * The fact is that interest and speculation are both made possible by the establishment of a false money system, the object of which is to make money scarce by restricting it within an artificial limit instead of allowing it its natural limit, as the Mutual Credit System proposes—the issue of secured credit in the form of certificates of credit (paper money), not on some special commodity of value, but on any and all commodities of value.

129 Such a volume of money as would result with this system would destroy speculation, because everyone would have an equal opportunity; while the mutual feature of the system would destroy interest (36-39). Interest, therefore, is not the origin of speculation, but both interest and speculation are the result of a monopoly of money.

130 In the following startling proposition, interest is calculated at the rate of 6 per cent: "Suppose one cent had been put at interest at the commencement of the Christian era, what would it have amounted to at simple, and what at compound interest, at the end of the year 1827?

Answer:

Simple, $1,186.20

Compound,

$172,616,474,047,552,529,470,760,914,974,711,959,976,620,354.56

nearly—a sum greater than could be contained in six millions of globes, each equal to our earth in magnitude and all of solid gold."—*Roswell C. Smith's Arithmetic, 1837.*

---

*The other point referred to will be found in paragraphs 315, 318.

"WE MUST HAVE GOVERNMENT."

131 Such a statement never came from a philosophical reasoner. It is manifestly absurd to say "we must have" of anything except those things that are indispesable to life, such as air, water, food, etc. Man's mode of life, his institutions, the means of satisfying his wants, and even the wants themselves, are ever changing. Those who have experimented in hygienic living know how superfluous are some of the "wants" it was their custom religiously to satisfy; and those who have become evolutionists realize how far man is from knowing what he really does want (need). Poor little pigmy! But a speck in the universe, tossed about on the great ocean of life; the sport of forces he does not comprehend; the victim of his own ignorance; this manikin, who boasts of a history, the philosophy of which he has yet to decipher; whose efforts at justice are a mockery; whose dominant propensity is free booty, and whose basis of ethics is, "heads, I win; tails, you lose"; this embodiment of hypocrisy and fraud; this Philistine, is presumptuous enough not only to have an opinion regarding morals, how we shall exchange commodities, which commodities are good for us and which are not; but this ignoramus has the audacity to incorporate his opinions into statutes and enforce them upon his unwilling fellow-beings. How does he know that he is right? There is no more certain indication of ignorance than the constant and persistent effort to enforce an opinion. To doubt is the very beginning of wisdom. If such people would only doubt as to the wisdom of the course they pursue, it would be an indication that they realize that possibly they might be wrong; but this is foreign to their nature. Their anxiety does not run in that direction. Their egotism

is ever rapaciously hankering for the exercise of authority. A little doubt as to the right to make the laws that have since been repealed, might have saved the cost of making and repealing them, the humiliation and ridicule they subjected us to, and the misery and injustice their enforcement entailed. These are the penalties, the burdens, that ignorance imposes on us. We remonstrate, and the only answer we can evoke is: "We must have government." A thesis of democracy is: "That government is best which governs least." This is proved to be true by the fact that the more government, the worse we are off. Laws multiply, and so does crime.

132 It may be hard for some people to realize that a very large part of mankind are Philistines, a sort of legal or conventional foot-pads, of whom we must be ever watchful in order that we may not be victimized in some way that we least expect. But what else do the records of the courts, if not our own immediate experience, teach us? Not only are we forever witnessing those acts that come under the category of crimes, but we are daily surprised by little acts of vantage which tell too plainly the motive. Such wide-spread cupidity! Cupidity that is alert on all occasions, and in every sphere of life; that stoops to all devices; that knows no bounds and will take any chances; is a sad commentary on the claims of paternalists and altruistic moralists.

133 One would naturally conclude that such results would induce inquiry into other methods of dealing with evils for which government is supposed to be a remedy, but of which it is an aggravation, and that those who suffer the most from these evils would be only too glad to examine any method that promised relief; but in spite of the admitted theory— that government is best which governs least,—the records of the past, and our own immediate experience, the superstition "we must have government" still dominates the minds of the masses, and appeals to reason are disregarded. In vain it is asked: Where is the history of the government that has ceased to be that was not tyrannical? Where is the govern-

ment that has endured that is not despotic?* What is over-
taking us here at the present time? Precisely what has over-
taken all nations—centralization of power, always accompan-
ied with increase of corruption, demoralization and revolution.
All this must have some rational explanation. It is an axiom,
I think nowhere disputed, that there is no effect without
adequate cause. To what cause, then, shall we ascribe these
results? No sooner does an individual undertake an earnest
study of these questions than he becomes a deserter; and
while he may not go forth and proclaim his change of front,
he ceases to co-operate, as formerly, with the enemies of liberty. What has taken place? Whence the change he has
undergone? He has become enlightened. He has informed
himself; whereas before he was ignorant. Is it not true,
also, that those who are the most zealous in maintaining the
present order of things and the most persistent opponents of
a change, have never made a conscientious study of the subject? They have merely taken it for granted that "we must
have government," and, therefore, what the government
ordains must be right.

134 Now, is it not natural to suppose that the same
result would follow in at least a large majority of cases, that,
as stated, has occurred in all those who have made a conscientious study of this subject? And would not such results
work a complete change in our social institutions? Have we
not, then, an answer to the question: "To what cause shall
we ascribe these results?" What else but prevailing ignorance? Additional evidence of ignorance is manifested in the
fear entertained by those who have never made a study of
the Anarchistic philosophy† as expounded by P. J. Proud-

---

*Those who have not, and care to look up the question, are re-
ferred to "A Vindication of Natural Society," by Edmund Burke;
"History of Civilization in England," by Thos. Henry Buckle; "Intel-
lectual Development of Europe," by John W. Draper; "Social Statics," by Herbert Spencer.

†"Anarchy—Want of government in a state,—an anarchy, a commonwealth without a head or government."—*Skeat's Etymological
Dictionary of the English Language.*

hon* and others,† that it means the prevention of anything like order or system; that since "government is to preserve order," the abolition of government must mean the inauguration of disorder. All this misunderstanding shows that they are ignorant of the fact that government, instead of being the preserver of order is the promoter of disorder. This has been demonstrated unanswerably by these authors. Far from opposing system and order, Anarchism teaches the only true way to have a permanently peaceful system of society; that the State is an invader of personal right, and that order can only be preserved by maintaining personal right—*liberty*. As Spencer has so clearly pointed out, the State—government—originated in brute force; and as Burke so eloquently shows, has perpetuated itself by the same means. He says: "In vain you tell me that artificial government is good, but

---

* . . . . "May not anarchy, which is a very great evil become a very great good? Such is the question raised by a celebrated writer, M. Proudhon, and he did not hesitate to answer it in the affirmative. If we understand him aright, the anarchy of M. Proudhon is nothing but self government carried to its extreme limits, and the last step in the progress of human reason. According to him, men will at last acknowledge that, instead of disputing and fighting over questions of which, in the majority of cases, they know nothing, and instead of seeking to enslave each other, they would do better to accept the law of labor frankly and join hands to triumph over the numerous obstacles which nature opposes to their well-being. In this new order of things, nations would be nothing more than groups of producers bound together by close ties of common interest. Politics, as hitherto understood, would have no further raison d'etre, and anarchy, that is to say, the disappearance of all political authority, would be the result of this transformation of human society in which all questions to be solved would have a purely economic character. Long ago J. B. Say advanced the opinion that the functions of the State should be reduced to the performance of police duties. If so reduced, there would be but one step needed to reach the an-archy of M. Proudhon.—suppression of the police power."—*L. Foubert, in Cyclopedia of Political Science, edited by John J. Lalor, 1883.*

†"What is Property" and "The Philosophy of Misery," by P. J. Proudhon; "True Civilization," by Josiah Warren; "Science of Society," by Stephen Pearl Andrews; "Yours or Mine" and "Hard Cash," by E. H. Heywood; "Instead of a Book," by Benj. R. Tucker, and his fortnightly paper, "Liberty"; and "The Anarchists," by John Henry Mackay.

that I fall out only with the abuse. The thing; *the thing itself* is the abuse!"

135   To say that these authors who have made the most critical analysis of all the factors that figure in our social relations; these men of keen intellect, who have shown up the errors and fallacies of the abettors of the methods of force, demonstrating that the recognition of the right of the individual to his person and property is the fundamental principle upon which a rational system of society must rest; these philosophers whose works have been ignored and excluded from the libraries in the vain hope of patching up and perpetuating that relic of the barbarous past, that despoiler of all that is good and noble in the race; that institution that is barren of any good whatever; the parent of all evil, the sum of all villainies—the State,—to say that these men want disorder; that they have no regard for private property and that what they aim at is a chaotic condition in which there will be no security to person or property, is the most inexcusable perversion of fact. From the right of the individual to his (or her) person and property, they argue the denial of the right of government to impose taxes, because it is the antithesis of the right to private property. Either the individual has a right to his property or he has not. If he has a right to his property, then, no one, not even government, can take it without his consent. It cannot take all of it, nor even a fraction of it; for a fraction of it is as much his as the whole of it is, and to take a fraction of it without his consent is as much a violation of the principle of right as to take the whole. This principle is so well recognized even in law, that anyone caught appropriating the property of another, however insignificant its value, is dealt with as having violated the right of private property.

136   Only government, within certain limits, can take property without the consent of the owner, with impunity. When it exceeds the limit, the people resist, even by the use of force if necessary. This in itself constitutes a denial of

the "right" of government, and shows that the people consent to be robbed up to a certain extent, because they do not
know what else to do. Here again is more evidence of popular ignorance. Upon this same principle of right,—the
right of the individual to his person—is based the denial of
the "right" of government to call upon the individual to bear
arms against his consent. If the individual has the right to
his person, he has the right at any and all times and under all
circumstances, to decide whether he will bear arms or not.
For if he has not the right to refuse to bear arms, then he
has not the right exclusively and absolutely to his person.

137 Having determined that these two constitute the
fundamental principles in social science, these philosophers
affirm with unfaltering assurance that the most desirable and
satisfactory state of society can be attained only through their
recognition and absolute inviolability; that such must necessarily be the result, and they proceed to demonstrate that it
would be the result.

138 Instead, therefore, of those who advocate the abolition of the State desiring a state of disorder, they prove that
it is the only possible way of attaining an orderly state of
society, and that the existence of the State is the main hindrance to its realization. That the statement, "we must have
government" should be changed to: WE MUST ABOLISH
GOVERNMENT.

139 But to the average man or woman, "we must abolish
government" is a scarecrow, a bugaboo of more hideous
proportions, if possible, than that sublime myth, the prince of
devils. What are they scared at? In the first place, there is
no hope that government will be abolished so long as people
are ignorant of the fact that it is the cause, the originator of
all their woes. It is perpetuated through ignorance; and it
fosters ignorance, just as the church does, in order that it
may perpetuate itself. The abolition of government, of the
State, is an impossibility, except as it outgrows its "usefulness"; except as other institutions come forward and do the

work that it makes a pretense of doing, and the people realize it. The abolition of government, therefore, should not be feared as an evil. Even those who, from lack of information on the subject regard the existence of the State as necessary, will consent to its abolition when there shall be no further use for it. Will anyone insist on having policemen patroling the streets long after arrests shall have ceased and invasions of persons and property shall be a thing of the past? If that time never comes, then the policeman will not be abolished and there is nothing to fear.

140 The thesis of the abolition of the State is this: Seeing that government is an evil, a mistake, that it does not do what it promises to do; that it is an aggravation of the disorders for which it is supposed to be a remedy; that it does not and cannot promote order and justice, but is itself a most effectual hindrance to their establishment; let us institute such other means as will in reality bring about justice and order in society; that, since government never did, does not, and, in the nature of things, cannot, let us organize and put into operation that which can and will accomplish the ends we desire. Such is the philosophy that is designated Anarchism; the best definition of which is, perhaps, *the absolute inviolability of person and property.*

141 It may be well here to point out the difference between the Anarchist and the bomb thrower. No worse than government itself, which uses dynamite and gatling guns, he is a deluded victim; nevertheless, a product of the very society that condemns him, and being stronger than he, survives while he perishes. Philosophical Anarchism condemns the method—force.* It is contrary to the definition,

---

*The Standard Dictionary's definition of Anarchism is: "The principles, practices, or characteristic spirit of Anarchists; the theory that all forms of government are wrong and unnecessary." The Century Dictionary says: "Anarchy—Specifically—2. A social theory which regards the union of order and the absence of all direct government of man by man as the political ideal; absolute individual liberty."

"the absolute inviolability of person and property," and impolitic: it can accomplish no good unless it is to give the unphilosophical writers of the press something to say and startle lazy plutocrats out of their dream of security, while conditions are as diabolical as they well can be.

1.42 But, it is asked, what do you propose to substitute? The idea is well nigh universal with the philosophical reformers that the first step towards a new and peaceful order of society is necessarily a release from the grip of the money power. This can be accomplished by taking the control of money entirely out of the hands of government.* The idea

---

*"The right of the individual to do as he pleases with his own is an axiom with us. Trespass alone limits this right, and provided one does not trespass, one may, by competition or otherwise, ruin one's neighbor. But notwithstanding our axiom, and notwithstanding we place little restriction upon this right, there is one thing individual may not, *must not*, do. One may freely fashion one's gold and silver into ring, watch, spoon, etc., and pass or sell at alleged weight and fineness, but one may not, *must not*, without crime, fashion into coin and pass or sell at alleged weight or fineness; and one may also freely issue and sell time promises to pay, but one may not, *must not*, without crime, issue and circulate demand promises to pay.

"Slightest thought should show the injustice and absurdity, and therefore injury of such prohibition; but as some cannot think, and many will not think, these perceive neither the injury, injustice nor absurdity; and as the few who do think qualify their perceptions with so many imaginary and impossible fears, they might as well not think. Hence, all unite in preventing individual doing as he pleases with his own, respecting coining money and issuing circulating promises to pay. All fear to permit right and leave consequences to righteous Nature, lest Nature stultify herself and bring evil out of good.

"To prevent right is to commit wrong. Now, what is government that it can righteously prevent one doing as one pleases with one's bullion and putting one's property into such shapes as one pleases? Government is not, as generally supposed, a mysterious, omnipotent creature, whose simple fiat makes right and wrong, but is merely an aggregate or collective individual. Aggregation of individuals into government does not impart to the aggregate a different nature from its component units, nor rights different in kind, however in degree, from said units—no more than aggregation of seeds of wheat until they fill an elevator changes the nature of the grain. Government differs from the individual only as the grains from the mass—that is in degree, not in nature. Now, as righteous individual cannot arbitrarily prevent individual doing as he pleases with his own, so neither can the aggregate individual, or government, righteously prevent its individual units."—*Right of Individual to Coin Money and Issue Notes,*" by *Lewis H. Blair.*

of the necessity for government supervision and regulation of
money, as the "Galveston News" puts it, "was borrowed
from the previous royal system." Royalty, wherever it has
existed, has availed itself of the opportunity which ignorance
on this subject afforded, and arrogated to itself the right to
provide and regulate the supply of money. But invasion of
personal liberty in many other instances has been regarded as
unwarranted interference; and in the establishment of government in this country, and since, much discussion has taken
place as to the proper sphere of government. Why has this
phase of the question escaped the careful examination it
deserves? Why is it that the popular writers and the press
generally take it for granted that it is a proper function of
government to dictate what shall be used as a medium of
exchange? It implies a belief not only in the wisdom, but in
the honesty of lawmakers that is at variance with all
experience.*

143   The history of the world is a history of corruption.
Listen to Tom Moore: "All the governments that I see or
know are a conspiracy of the rich, who, on pretense of manag-
ing the public only pursue their private ends, devise ways
and means to preserve all that they have so ill acquired; then
to engage the poor to toil for them at as low rates as possible
and oppress them as much as they please."—*Tom Moore's
Utopia.*

"Like loaded dice by ministers are thrown,
    And each new set of sharpers cog their own;
Hence the rich oil that from the Treasury steals,
    Drips smooth o'er all the Constitution's wheels,
Giving the old machine such pliant play
    That Courts and Commons jog one joltless way,
While Wisdom trembles for the crazy car,
    So gilt, so rotten, carrying fools so far;

---

*The reader is recommended to read "Seven Financial Conspira-
cies," by Mrs. S. E. V. Emery.

And the duped people, hourly doomed to pay
The sums that bribe their liberties away,—
Like the young eagle, who has lent his plume
To fledge the shaft by which he meets his doom,—
See their own feathers plucked to wing the dart
Which rank corruption destines for their heart."
—*From Tom Moore's Poem on Corruption.*

THE ALLIANCE AND PROHIBITORY FINANCIAL LAW.

[*From the Galveston News.*]

144   The Alliance is an offspring of certain oppressive conditions, and the Alliance will sooner appreciate the truth of what the *News* has been saying regarding repressive, prohibitory paternalism than will certain benevolent gentlemen in the old parties, who are paternal in their solicitude to prevent the people from hurting themselves in and by economic liberty.   It is not likely that the Alliance would ever have gone to the government for issues of currency if the government had left banking business as free as the boot-making and grocery business.   The people either know how much credit and currency they need or they are not competent to manage their own business affairs.   Prohibitory paternalism envelops everything in such a cloud that gentlemen like Senator Reagan are astonished to hear that which they never suspected—that they are paternalists, as proved by the test of what they desire to forbid.   At least if they are willing to have bankers, and farmers and other producers come together and arrange for the issue of all the secured currency which property owners desire to have manufactured and to pay for in a free market, they give no sign, but often intimate that the property owner will be ruined if the law allows him to pledge his property different from now.   How bitter a satire to the Alliance farmer this is!   He is free to borrow monopoly money on all but his homestead, and pay 10 per cent. The interest may eat him up.   He learns that a different currency, merely representative of wealth, can be made and secured, and of course its cost is nothing like the interest which currency commands as now known—a mere addendum to monopoly money.   The borrower being an owner of wealth, currency to render that wealth fluid, mobile, is what

he needs, and the proper price to pay is what it costs (97). No better taught, he looks to government (305). He is met even by Democrats in the spirit of a sincere, ignorant, repressive paternalism, with something like this: "Dear boys, you would pledge your property and overdo the thing; make mistakes, and your property would pass into other hands." As much caution and advice as gentlemen in political life like, but the Alliance is right as to all but the goverment being the warehouser and banker, and it is coming to this, that the Democratic party must show whether it is in favor of liberty in finance. The owners of values would have long ago combined to supply themselves with currency which need not cost more than 1 per cent and be perfectly good, but prohibitory law stands in the way. The Alliance has come to demand through government what government has wrongfully forbidden to come into being naturally. Wherever government strikes down trade the demand will come that government itself do the thing needed if it will not let private parties do it. The *News* has used Senator Reagan as an illustration, but its criticism applies to the majority of other statesmen who consider themselves opposed to paternalism. It tells them candidly that they cannot grapple with the Alliance until they come to a platform of economic liberty on the currency question as in all else. It is a necessary alternative. The people will have currency, and will not pay for it a rental entirely disproportioned to its cost of manufacture and control, when they furnish the wealth as security. There is nothing else essentially in the question, delicate and difficult as it may be, than security and management. What the Democrats should be about as to the money question, is to take reason of the Alliance and give it an antipaternal form and issue. Not that the Alliance might at once accept free banking. Paternalism has brooded and reigned too long to abdicate at once from the minds of men. But this is the alternative, and the only alternative (145-147).

144a   The foregoing is an editorial, and the *Galveston News* is the ablest and most influential daily paper in the state of Texas. It has for some years past been an advocate and an able defender of freedom in the supply of money

145   Mr. Lewis H. Blair, in his very able essay, "Standard of Value," says: "We are so accustomed to the regulative,

but especially restrictive, hand of government in things monetary, we can scarcely conceive of any monetary system based on liberty and competition. Many objections, therefore, will immediately and spontaneously arise to the proposition that government must absolutely dissociate itself from coinage and currency. The chief and most formidable will be that it is the duty of government to protect the citizens against bad money. We shall examine only this objection, because if this is found baseless all other objections fall with it.

146 "It is denied that it is the duty of the government to protect the citizen against bad money. The duty of the government is simply to protect him in his life, liberty and pursuit of happiness. In all other respects—in his food, raiment, shelter, business, religion, etc.—he is, or should be, left to look out for himself, and when so left he protects himself better than government can, and so it should and would be with money.

147 "A universal currency is a great desideratum, but such currency can never be until monetary matters are entirely dissociated from government and left to the free play of conflicting interests. When thus dissociated and left to intelligent self-interest, not a generation will probably pass before the great financial interests of civilization will have agreed upon a universal coinage, varying only in appearance and nomenclature, co-extensive with commerce. A universal currency resting upon consent and not arbitrary statute would only be an extension of the clearing-house systems of London, New York, and other great financial centers. These have arisen naturally and do their work perfectly, and in like manner a universal currency would as naturally arise and do its work perfectly, if government would restrain its regulative hand."

148 It should be borne in mind that the abolition of government is only an extension of that degree of liberty attained in the consummation of American independence. If we rejoice at the progress thus far made towards human liberty, why should we deprecate still further progress? To advocate the abolition of government is simply to favor such measures as will bring about conditions under which no government will be necessary. Herbert Spencer says: "It is a mistake to assume that government must necessarily last

forever. The institution marks a certain stage of civilization
—is natural to a particular phase of human development.   It
is not essential but incidental." * Those who oppose the abolition of government are, logically, in favor of a continuance of
crime and policemen to arrest the criminals.   The choice is
between prosperity and the inviolability of person and property, or poverty and the policeman's club; and our opponents
virtually say, "we want poverty and the policeman's club."

149   The story of him whom the Christians worship can
all be told in these few words: In a certain nation there
appeared before the public a peaceful and inoffensive citizen,
who said: "I can show you how you can all become happy."
And straightway a few of the prominent and wealthy men
said among themselves: "This man wants to overthrow our
institutions that we have reared; let us hang him."   And
they went and hung him.   So it appears to be now—not a
question of whether we would be happier by any proposed
change, but, is it likely to affect our institutions.   To perpetuate these is the real purpose of government, while progress
is constantly demanding their abolition as things we have
outgrown.   As evidence of the persistence with which it
inflicts them upon the people, let the following from the
Westminster Review testify.   And let the reader bear in
mind while perusing this history of money panics in England,
that the sublime folly that caused them (the monopoly of the
Bank of England), was the culmination of discussions in
which participated the "wisest" and most famous men of the
time.   Mr. A. J. Warner, in his statement before the Committee on Banking and Currency, December 14, 1894, said:
"Probably no question in which the public is concerned ever
underwent so thorough a discussion as this question of the
regulation of currency, not only in this country, but particularly in Great Britain from 1810 down to 1857.   Every phase
of the question was discussed over and over again.   Parlia-

* "Social Statics," page 24.   Edition of 1890.

mentary commission after commission was established to consider every proposition presented. First came the celebrated
bullion report of 1810, then the report of the secret commission of 1819, then the commission of 1826, that of 1840, and
finally of 1857, in which was summed up, in my judgment,
the wisdom of the entire discussion, and to the discussion which
then took place, so far as I know, nothing really has been
added since that time. I believe that the general conclusions
then reached have been accepted by all writers of distinction
from that day down to this." The following articles are a
history of the effects produced by the institution approved by
these "writers of distinction" and instituted by the government.

STATE TAMPERING WITH MONEY AND BANKS.

[*Westminster Review, Jan., 1858.*]

150 When, in 1793, there came a general crash, mainly
due to an unsafe banking system which had grown up in the
provinces *in consequence* of the Bank of England monopoly—
when the pressure, extending to London, had become so great
as to alarm the bank directors and cause them suddenly to
restrict their issues, thereby producing a frightful multiplication of bankruptcies, the government (to mitigate an evil
indirectly produced by legislation) determined to issue
Exchequer Bills to such as could give adequate security.
That is, they allowed hard-pressed citizens to mortgage their
fixed capital for an equivalent of State promises to pay with
which to liquidate demands on them. The effect was magi-
cal. . . . . . In 1825 again, when the bank of England, after having intensified a panic by extreme restriction
of its issues, suddenly changed its policy and in four days
advanced 5,000,000*l* notes on all sorts of securities, the panic
at once ceased (page 214). And now mark two important
truths; one of them, indeed, already indicated in the foregoing paragraph. Observe, in the first place, that this expansion of paper circulation which naturally takes place in times
of impoverishment or commercial difficulty, is highly salutary.
This issuing of securities for future payment when there does
not exist the wherewith for immediate payment is a means of

mitigating national disasters that would else be far more severe·
In a few words, the process amounts to a postponement of
trading engagements that cannot at once be met.   And the
alternative questions to be asked respecting it are,—shall the
merchants, manufacturers, shop-keepers, etc., who, by unwise
investments, or war, or famine, or great lossess abroad, have
been in part deprived of the means of meeting the claims
upon them, be allowed to mortgage their fixed capital to a
bank in return for promises to pay of equivalent value? or
by being debarred from so issuing memoranda of claims on
their fixed capital, shall they be made bankrupt?   On the
other hand, if, as they must also be, they are forthwith made
bankrupt, carrying with them others, and these, again, others,
there follows in the first place, a most disastrous loss to all
creditors; property to an immense amount being peremptor-
ily sold at a time when there are comparatively few able to
buy, must go at a great sacrifice. . . . .

FREE TRADE IN BANKING.

[*Westminster Review, Jan., 1888.*]

151   It has become proverbial that men usually attribute
the sufferings they endure to any cause but the right one.
This tendency was never more strikingly realized than in the
present disposition to attribute the commercial depression of
recent times to free trade—to over-production and to foreign
competition—and this, regardless of the fact that foreign
nations are suffering equally with ourselves.   Those who
reason thus little dream that, except to a very limited extent,
free trade has never been tried, and that therefore it cannot
have proved a failure.   While the oppressive and costly system of indirect taxation and the disastrous monopoly of money
remain, it is perfectly idle to talk of free trade having been
tried in this* or any other country.   The principle is right—
perfect freedom of exchange between nations and individuals
—and what is needed is simply to carry it out.

152   It is the monopoly of the banking system to which
we propose to call attention in the present paper.   Our object
will be to show that the English bank and currency laws,

---

* The *Westminster Review* is an English magazine.

and especially the Bank Act of 1844, have been most disastrous in their influence on industry and commerce, and that they are, at the present moment a most influential cause of the long-continued and wide-spread depression which all lament.

153   This subject was exhaustively treated in the January number of this *Review* for 1858; and many clear thinkers had at that time denounced the existing system, but the effort failed to arouse public attention sufficiently to ensure a remedy; and subsequent events have formidably aggravated the evil, rendering it imperative now to reiterate the expose of this gigantic wrong, with a view to its speedy removal.

154   *It is impossible to over-estimate the importance of an abundance and regular supply of money. It is absolutely essential to that freedom of exchange on which healthy commerce and national well-being depend.* [Italics mine.] But our bank laws have rendered these conditions impossible by arbitrary and wholly unjustifiable interference with the conditions of supply and demand which affect money precisely as they affect every other commodity. . . . . Not only has the supply been needlessly restricted, but that restriction has been so capricious, so frequent, so sudden and so extreme, that panic and commercial disaster have followed to an incalculable extent.

155   The Bank of England was established in 1694, and on free trade principles.   It was a joint-stock company, and it commenced its operations with a loan to the government, then very much pressed for money to carry on a war with France.   Patterson, its intelligent founder, had no idea whatever of its having any monopoly or special privilege, but he soon ceased to be one of its directors, and in 1708, only fourteen years after its establishment, the government, in return for another loan, passed a law that no other joint-stock bank should remain in England.   The result was the establishment of a large number of small banks which, unable to stand against the intensely selfish manipulations of the government *protege*, perished in numbers in every commercial crisis and rendered a safe system of banking impossible.

156   It was not until 1826 that the government partly reversed this mischievous policy and permitted the establishment of joint-stock banks in England.   Even now they are not allowed to issue any notes, though their subscribed capital and reserve fund, taken together, are many times greater than those of the Bank of England.

157   The worst evils of the monopoly of the Bank of England were not felt till the present century.   Towards the close of the last century, the wars in which we were engaged drained the national resources, and exhausted the ingenuity of Mr. Pitt in the endeavor to raise the "sinews of war."   The transition was frequent from increased imposts on commodities to income tax, and from that to enormous loans to be paid in some indefinite future, under the burden of which we now groan.   But all would not avail, not even with the iniquitous redemption of the land tax—that last attempt to free land from all responsibility and to throw the whole burden of taxation on the people.   But even this would not serve and in 1793 specie payment was suspended and the currency was entirely carried on by paper money until specie payment was resumed in 1819.   The conclusion of the war naturally caused great changes in commercial affairs.   Corn had been grown at home during its continuance, prices had been high and rents had risen.   But when foreign corn was admitted, prices fell and rents could not be maintained.   To keep up rents without ruin to farmers the corn laws were imposed in 1816 and the burden of taxation was still further thrown upon the people.

158   But to aggravate the evil a stupendous change was made the same year in the currency laws, fraught with untold mischief—the demonetization of silver.   Up to that time silver and gold had been alike legal tender and together they had been far from sufficient for the requirements of the nation.   Gold had been 110s. per ounce, its nominal price being 77s. 10d.   Panic and ruin had prevailed in the three previous years, 1814-15-16; ninety provincial banks having become bankrupt and as many more having been dissolved; and yet our infatuated rulers must needs increase the evil infinitely more by decreeing in 1816 that silver should no longer be a legal tender beyond the amount of 40s.

159   The infatuation of this step it is impossible to appreciate or account for.   Continual scarcity of money had produced the same disastrous results.   There was a panic from this cause in 1793 and it could only be relieved by the issue of £5,000,000 in Exchequer bills and in 1811 a similar crisis occurred which was relieved by the same means.

160   In 1819, with gold the only legal tender and the supply of money thus artificially limited, the government returned to cash payments and at the same time materially

restricted the paper currency. To intensify this evil, they lent £30,000,000 of gold to the French government, and, still worse, the supply of gold from the American mines had materially fallen off. The consequence was a depression of trade and general distress and ruin terrible to contemplate. The attempted remedy was monstrous. Instead of an increased paper issue, this was still further contracted and discounts were restricted, in order to bring gold from abroad. Though the directors of the Bank of England told the government that the act would ruin the great body of the people, it was passed. Up to 1819 the supply of precious metals had sunk to one-half, at the same time that the trade of the country had immensely increased. These measures were followed in 1826 by one of the most disastrous panics the world has ever witnessed. Alison in his great history dwells emphatically upon the ruinous results of the diminished supply of the precious metals from the American mines combined with the contraction of the currency in our own country. As in the present crisis, the effect of this mischievous policy was attributed to a wrong cause, and demands were made for protection against importation from foreign lands. The panic of 1826 was caused entirely by the capricious action of the bank authorities. For some years they increased their circulation of paper money, and then, finding their stock of gold nearly exhausted, they suddenly diminished the note circulation to the extent of £3,-500,000. A general distrust took the place of undue confidence which had pervaded the country; the notes of the country banks were returned upon them to such a degree that a great number failed and a "run" upon many London bankers ensued, followed by the stoppage of several. Commercial distress of the most frightful description followed, and such was the loss of confidence that the wealthiest merchants were driven to make heavy sacrifices of property, in order to make provision for their immediate engagements. To use the memorable expression of Mr. Huskison, "the country was within twenty-four hours of barter." The remedy was found in again increasing the paper currency. The bank had caused the panic by limiting the circulation to save itself. It increased the paper circulation again and the panic ceased. Between November 3rd and December 29th, the amount of mercantile bills under discount increased from £4,000,000 to £15,000,000; the number of bills discounted

6

in one particular day being 4,200.   The effort thus made
was assisted by one circumstance, purely accidental.   A box
containing £1 notes which had been overlooked when the
bank called in all its notes under £5, was discovered just in
time, and, in the opinion of Mr. Harmon, one of the directors, the timely issue of these notes "worked wonders; it
saved the credit of the country."   Between December 3rd
and 31st the bank-notes in circulation were increased from
£17,000,000 to £25,000,000.   This great increase was necessary to replace the notes of the country bankers that had
suddenly been withdrawn from circulation, and to counteract
the tendency to hoarding always indulged in by timid persons in periods of embarassment.   Foreign exchanges again
turned in our favor and the gold forced abroad by previous
mismanagement came back.

161   The next foolish step taken by the government was
in 1829 when all notes for less than £5 were made illegal in
England.   It was proposed to apply this law to Scotland,
but the sagacity of Sir Walter Scott saved Scotland from the
calamity, and she enjoys the circulation of her £1 notes to
this day.

162   From this time a panic seems to have occurred about
once in ten years, and partial ones more frequently, always
traceable to scarcity of money arising from the peculiar liability of gold to be withdrawn to other countries.   In 1837
one of these crises occurred after three or four years of comparative prosperity, occasioned by the despotic action of
President Jackson in the United States forbidding bank-
notes to be recognized as legal tender, and requiring all payments to the government to be made in gold and silver.
Trade was checked in the States, interest rose to 24 per cent
and a large drain of gold from England followed.   The
Bank of England raised the discount to 6 per cent and borrowed £2,000,000 from Parisian bankers.   English trade
suffered severely.

163   It is strange, beyond conception, that the disasters
resulting from the note circulation and rate of discount
being dependent upon the amount of gold in the bank, did
not lead to some effectual remedy.   On the contrary, the
infatuation was so complete, that from this time, the bank
stereotyped in the act of 1844 this ruinous system, leaving
the trade of England at the mercy of every foreign power,
and producing one disastrous crisis after another.

164 From 1840 to 1843 an influx of Russian gold gave some relief to commerce. This gold, the product of Russian mines, had hitherto been allowed to lie in the bank coffers of Russia. It was now employed in the purchase of government stocks in the west of Europe and especially in the British funds. In 1843 the bullion in the Bank of England was £16,000,000—four times the average since 1831. The Bank Act of 1844, however, neutralized the advantages that should have arisen from the influx of Russian gold; it allowed no increased issue of notes except those of the Bank of England; it limited the issue of that bank, causing the amount to be determined by the amount of gold in its cellars, and did not allow even the Bank of Scotland to issue any unless it retained in its coffers an equal amount of gold.*

165 Sir Robert Peel well knew the far-reaching effect of any alteration in the currency laws, but he was totally blind to the real nature of the act which he introduced. Instead of being alive to the disastrous effects of the act of 1819, he described that of 1844 as merely the complement of it, and he perpetuated its worst features in an aggravated form. Its two great evils are: 1, the extreme liability to disturbance from the regulations with regard to gold; 2, the capricious and arbitrary limitations of the paper currency.

166 The principal provisions of the Bank Charter are briefly these:† 1. That after 1844 no new bank should be permitted to issue bank-notes and that no bank whatever should issue a note in London or within sixty-five miles of London, except, of course, the Bank of England.

167 2. The banks enjoying the right of issue previous to 1844 should be forbidden to extend it, whatever may be the future expansion of their business.

168 3. That a fixed amount of £14,000,000 in notes might in future be issued by the Bank of England against a like amount lent to the government by the bank. All further issues to be covered by bullion, of which not exceeding one-fourth may be silver. This last provision is utterly useless, since millions of silver may not pay one £5 note.

169 4. In case of private banks ceasing to issue notes, the Queen in Council may authorize the bank to increase its note issues by two-thirds of the amount so withdrawn.

* Paterson's "New Golden Age."
†"Financial Reformer Almanac," 1885.

170   In 1855 this power was exercised and further note issues of £475,000 against stock were sanctioned, such being two-thirds of their discontinued private issues.

171   A somewhat similar arrangement followed with regard to the Bank of Ireland and special provisions were permitted for Scotland.   But in both countries the amount of circulation was closely restricted.   No new banks of issue were permitted and in consequence no new bank has been established in this country, so far as we know.

172   The following are some of the effects of this Bank Act: The number of banks enjoying the petty right of a fixed issue has steadily decreased from £9,750,000, forty-four years ago, to £3,250,000 in 1883.   On the other hand, the Bank of England, whose whole note issue was £15,750,000 in 1840 (that is, six millions above theirs), was £25,000,000 in 1883, or twenty-three and three-fourths millions above theirs.   The total inadequacy of this note issue to the requirements of the country is proved by a recent statement from the *Economist* to the effect that the note circulation in England in 1844 was over 20*s.* per head of the population and is now under 10*s.* per head.   The imports and exports of Britain per head in 1854 were £9 14*s.* and in 1886 £20 4*s.*   The currency is thus reduced to one-sixth as compared to the work to be done.

173   The only proof required of the utter rottenness of the Bank Act of 1844 is found in the fact that on three occasions,—namely, in 1847, 1857 and 1866—its operation has been suspended by government, *not* to relieve commercial distress, *but to save the bank from stopping payment.* Immediate relief and cessation of panic have in every case followed its suspension; proving beyond question that the crisis was artificial and unnecessary,—created, in fact, by the law itself.

174   The panic in 1847 began by failures in the corn trade.   Wheat fell from 120*s.* to 60*s.* the quarter.   Then several banks failed: the general complaint was want of money.   The bank rate was raised from 3 to 7¼ per cent and panic followed.   The pressure continued, with ruin on every hand until the government authorized the bank to issue more notes than the law allowed.   The effect was immediate.   Confidence was restored.   Hoarded notes were brought out and discounts were everywhere readily obtained. £7,500,000 of bullion had left the bank and notes had conse-

quently been diminished to that extent. The bank advanced £4,000,000 in one day in sums of from £300,000 to £50,000 to different banks and London houses. The panic ceased, but the number of tradespeople irretrievably ruined and the wide-spread misery will never be told.

175 The crisis of 1857 began with extensive failures in America from over speculation in railways, land, etc., resulting in failures in England. The drain of gold was such that on the 12th November, with discount at 10 per cent, the total reserve in the bank was only £384,144 and at its branches £196,607 more. The bankers' claims alone against it were £5,458,000. It is clear, therefore, that but for the suspension of the act the bank must have stopped. Thousands by this time had been ruined. An order in council again authorized an extensive issue of bank-notes and the panic ceased. £6,776,000 were issued beyond the limit fixed by the act. No further proof is required of the utter rottenness of the act than the fact that it required to be suspended and its mode of operation entirely reversed, within three years after its enactment and twice more within twenty years. It was after this terrible crisis that Mr. Gladstone said: "The act cannot stand as it is. I cannot consent that the law shall be suspended at intervals to meet these constantly recurring crises. The act was damaged in 1847. It was shattered in 1857."

176 And yet thirty years have elapsed and this ruinous act is in operation still and it is steadily precipitating the nation into commercial ruin and social and political confusion. Prices are steadily going down, investments are becoming unprofitable, all fixed charges, including rents, salaries, mortgages, wages and taxes are becoming more burdensome every day. Trade is being carried on at a loss; and all this that the monopolist bank may enrich its proprietors by the ruin of the nation.* Wages are coming down, but too slowly to save employers from ruin. The trades unions are most unwilling to submit to any reduction, though their members benefit by the low prices that prevail. The purchasing power of what they earn is two or three times what it was a few years ago, yet they will go on strike rather than submit to a ten per cent reduction.

---

* Precisely the same effect that monopoly of money has produced in this country.

177   That such would be the effect of the Bank Act of 1844 was clearly seen by some of its most ardent supporters. Lord Ashburton, one of its prime champions, said: "Our monetary laws put it in the power of a few shrewd capitalists so to contract the supply of gold as to embarrass the bank and nearly ruin the nation." Lord Overstone, another advocate of the system, said: "Against the actual exhaustion of its treasures through foreign exchange, the bank has the power of protecting itself. But to do this she must produce a pressure upon the money market ruinous for its suddenness and severity. She must save herself by the ruin of all around her."

178   The result has proved, as we have shown, the baselessness of the first part of this latter declaration; for without its illegal suspension on three several occasions, the bank would have become insolvent. The latter statement as to the ruin of all around her is too true, as thousands have proved to their cost.

179   The third illegal suspension of the act was in 1866. On this occasion, over-trading and fictitious credit helped to bring on the crisis, but many perfectly solvent firms were involved in the ruin, because in the panic they could not meet the unprecedented demand put upon them. The Bank of England could do nothing to help them though it had plenty to do it with; it could not, as the law stood, convert its assets into currency (bank-notes). When, by an order in council allowed to do it, the panic ceased. No less than £4,000,000 were allowed in one day—altogether, £5,000,000.

180   Before the passing of the Bank Act of 1844, the bank rate rarely varied more than one or two per cent. The following figures, including the period of the last illegal suspensions, will give some idea of the suddenness, extent and caprice of its fluctuations since 1844.

BANK RATE OF DISCOUNT.

Years	Per cent	Per cent	No. of changes each year
1862		2 Aug. and Sept.	5
1864	3½ in May	7½ Sept.	6
1865	6 March	9 Sept.	9
1866	10 June, July	3½ Dec.	10
1867	3½ Jan.	2 Aug. to end	3

181   Beginning at 2 per cent in 1862, the rate gradually, though irregularly rises till it obtains its maximum of 10 per

cent in June, 1866, the very time of the crisis; from which time it falls rapidly until, in a little more than a year, it is at its minimum of 2 per cent again. Observe, too, the number of changes, from five to ten in a single year. No wonder that trade is depressed and that commercial panics are frequent with such manipulations of the monopolist bank!

182 The following extract from the *Financial Reformer* of January, 1886, is a fresh illustration of this gigantic evil. "The bank rate was doubled again, within a little more than a month—namely, from 2 to 4 per cent, and this not, as far as appears, from any revival of business, and consequently increased healthy demand for credit, but only, as usual, from some light export of gold; so that for a cause really in no way arising from or indirectly concerning the general trade of the country, traders are, as we have several times pointed out, taxed without their consent, at the rate of £100,000,000 a year—which is, nevertheless, taken quite as a matter of course—newspapers and Chambers of Commerce uttering never a word of complaint, notwithstanding general stagnation and failure of profit. If Parliament were to impose by law an extra tax of one-tenth the amount, it would make an outcry throughout the three kingdoms. But the Bank Act may do what mischief it will. People do not, and apparently will not take the trouble to understand its operations and so they continue to suffer. It is beyond question that the bank monopoly and the act of 1844 are a principal cause of depression in business; and equally certain, in our opinion, that nothing like permanent or steady prosperity can exist while they continue. All our forty years of experience of them proves this most abundantly; but for some inscrutable reason, John Bull prefers to go on suffering, instead of 'putting himself to school' on this question and learning to understand what is no such really difficult matter, after all."

183 These well-marked crises which occur once in ten years or oftener are not the only evil of our hidebound currency. They may be regarded as the acute form of the disease. But there is a chronic malady not less formidable nor less threatening to the permanent welfare of the nation. The supply of gold and silver has long been inadequate to the requirements of commerce. Even with all the forms of paper currency still the gold produced has been insufficient for the growing wants of the world. We have seen how the flow of gold from Russia in 1840-43 was neutralized by the

Bank Act of 1844. The depression of prices continued without abatement until the discovery of the gold fields of Cali-
fornia in 1848 and of Australia in 1851, poured into Europe
an unprecedented supply of gold, at once relieving the prevailing distress and inaugurating a quarter of a century of
prosperity to which the world's history presents no parallel.
Up to this point, even the repeal of the corn laws had done
nothing to improve trade. Food had been placed within the
reach of starving thousands, but the first effect on agriculture
was injurious rather than beneficial and prices of all kinds
remained ruinously low.

184   From 1846 to 1851 the times were at their worst.
Farmers and manufacturers suffered alike, while low wages
and lack of employment fell heavily on the working classes.
But when the gold began to pour into Europe from Califor-
nia and Australia, it immediately gave relief to trade at home
and it gave a powerful impulse to industry, giving employment to shipping and every other department of trade. Ten
millions sterling were made annually at the diggings in Australia and the farmers worked the land, so that the gold col-
onies steadily increased in wealth. An immense trade sprang
up which greatly benefited this and other countries, giving
lucrative employment to thousands. From this time wages
rose and prices of all commodities advanced steadily and an
era of prosperity set in such as the world had never witnessed before. Alison, the historian, in view of these facts,
called the gold discovery "a currency extension act of nature."

185   At one time it was apprehended that the supply of
gold would be too great, and that an injurious reaction would
follow. M. Chevalier, a distinguished French economist,
wrote a book warning the world of this apprehended event.
But the apprehension was groundless. Two events con-
curred to prevent the catastrophe. The one was the falling
off of the gold supply to a much smaller annual production
than at first; the other was the absorption of silver in the
Indian and Chinese trade; the new gold taking the place of
the silver sent to the east. France alone absorbed £100,000,-
000 worth of gold in this way. To these may be added the
fact of Germany having adopted a gold standard in 1873
and having been followed in that course by several of the
European nations, thus still further enhancing the price of
gold. At the same time, since the discovery of silver in
Nevada, the supply of silver was naturally increased till now

the difference in value between the two is no less than 14 per cent. Several other European States have since followed the example of Germany in repudiating a silver currency,—all tending to aggravate the evil and rendering possible the most disastrous disturbance of commercial relations throughout the world.

186 This discrepancy affects most injuriously all our commercial relations with India. The normal value of silver is 60*d*. per ounce. It is now only worth 49*d*. or about four-fifths of its proper value. India has yearly to remit to England £15,000,000 which must here be paid in gold, so that more silver has to be remitted to make up for its depreciation. But the purchasing power in India remains and therefore, by the aid of Council drafts corn is purchased in India and sent over to this country instead of coin. From the same cause, the purchase of goods in England is discouraged, because Indian silver buys less than gold and less of those articles which have to be paid for in gold. So the tendency is to encourage exports from India but to discourage imports. With every fall in the price of silver wheat exports from India increase; with every rise in silver, they are checked; so that the English farmer is actually paying a bonus on Indian wheat at the rate of 5*s*. 4*d*. a quarter. For the same reason, English manufactures are checked. Indian silver will buy just so much less of English goods as the difference in value between gold and silver—a monstrous injustice alike to British manufacturers and to farmers, and to our Indian fellow-subjects.*

187 The gross injustice and oppression of the repudiation of silver as a legal tender is further illustrated by its effect on the national debt. In the year 1816 that debt amounted to £850,000,000 sterling. But the demonetization of silver converted it into a debt of 850,000,000 gold sovereigns. The effect of that change, now that gold is 14 per cent more valuable than it was in 1816, is to increase the debt by £100,000,000 and the interest which the tax-payer has to pay every year by more than £2,000,000. With every rise in the price of gold, this burden will press more heavily.

188 The currency question is very generally avoided, under the impression that it is so very complicated that none but accomplished experts can have an opinion of it. But,

---

* Moreton Frewer.

like every great question, though many of its details are
complicated and embarrassing, there is a way of looking at it
which will enable every person of average capacity and
knowledge to form a practical conclusion on the subject.   In
the foregoing pages stupendous evils have been exhibited
and traced to their true cause—the arbitrary interference of
the government with the law of supply and demand, in relation to bank-notes and to gold and silver.   We simply
require free trade in money, instead of the monopoly and the
privileged manipulations of the monopolist Bank of England.
The reform needed comprises palpably two particulars:

189   1.   Free trade principles must be applied to bank-
notes.   Every bank must be at liberty to issue them according to its means and requirements as men in other business
are left to decide for themselves the amount of credit they
shall seek to obtain—the sole condition required by the government being that they shall pay in coin on demand the
value of every note (323, 326, 330).   The disasters of the
past, which have thrown discredit on this principle, have
been caused by the government releasing bankers from this
responsibility and authorizing an inconvertible paper currency.   If left to the natural operation of supply and demand
the issue of bank-notes will be healthy and dishonest speculators will speedily meet their deserts.

190   2.   The fatal step taken in the demonetization of
silver must be retraced.   Silver must again be admitted as a
legal tender (341) to an unlimited extent, as it was before
the fatal departure of 1816, confirmed and aggravated as it
has been in its ruinous influence by the Banking Act of 1844.

191   Till these changes have been effected and fairly tried,
let no one exclaim against free trade as the cause of commercial depression.   Let the banking system be rendered commensurate with the wants of the nation and placed in harmony with the teachings of common sense and experience,
and then will dawn upon our country such an era of steady
commercial prosperity as has never hitherto been realized
except in the dreams of Utopia.

192 If two individuals living near each other, one of them having a well, and no other water is accessible—if the owner of the well should exact service from the other in exchange for the water which he allows him to take from the well, it is in no sense monopoly. But if an artificial restriction in the shape of a statute or municipal act should prohibit the man who has no well from digging one or catching rain water, then there would be monopoly. There would not be equal opportunity. Not being allowed to supply himself, he is dependent upon the other in consequence of this artificial restriction. If there are no restrictions, the one who has no well could dig one at his leisure and thus free himself from the exactions of his neighbor.

193 It is necessary to distinguish between natural disadvantages and artificial restrictions. Whatever natural disadvantages or obstacles Nature has put in the way of our comfort, are burdens we must avoid, overcome or endure. They are not designed or put in the way of some for the benefit of others, and we are all liable to stumble onto more than an equal share of them. In this we have to take our chances. Artificial restrictions are quite different. They are the work of man; are especially designed for the benefit of some, and cannot, in the very nature of things, be otherwise than disadvantageous to others; yet, while it is an accepted theory that no one has a right to benefit himself at the expense of another without that other's consent, such is the nature of our money system that a comparative few absorb the surplus earnings of all the rest without their consent; and it is done by means of artificial restrictions which limit the volume of money and consequently the volume of capital, thus increas-

ing profits to capital and interest on money, and diminishing
compensation to labor in the same proportion; for, as you
cannot take something from nothing, so, whatever the capitalist or money-lender acquires as compensation for the use
of capital or money, is taken from labor without adequate
return.

194 Monopoly of the medium of exchange is the most
cruel of all monopolies, because it is the basis of all monopoly.* There is no monopoly known to modern society that
would not succumb to the effects of free money. Take, for
instance, that which results from the tax on imports. Free
money, or the absence of all legislative interference with the
supply of money, would result in a supply of capital equal to
any demand there might be for it. It would be supplied
wherever needed, and in constantly increasing quantity and
ever diminishing rates of interest until cost was reached.
Since money could be obtained under the Mutual Credit System on good security, at one-half of one per cent per annum,
compensation to the capitalist for the use of his capital would
not long exceed that rate, or, as just stated, *cost.*

195 Such a revolution in affairs would utterly destroy the
conditions that demanded the tariff. Free trade in money so

---

* "The world's prices are fixed in the market of Liverpool by reference to gold. This is particularly in the interest of gold-owners,
bondholders, and money-lenders of England, for they control her
laborers, and by her industrial powers the world. Their strong arm
is the Bank of England. The Manchester Chamber of Commerce in
their report of 1859, refers to it in the following language: 'That its
directors, twenty-six in number, can, in secret session, without the
consent of their constituents, decide the value of all property, is one
of the greatest crimes against civilization.' 'How do you maintain
your supply of gold?' was asked by a parliamentary committee in
1847. 'By contracting our circulating notes, causing a decline of
prices and consequently an influx of gold,' was the answer. Again
they remarked: 'There is no means of supplying the bank with gold
except by diminishing the bank-notes, which immediately contracts
the currency and lowers prices by increasing the value of money.' .
. . . . The banking association controls all credit, and by this
means the revenues of all semi-public industries and the great national resources. Capitalism dominates production and the producers
have not yet learned to organize for their own defense."—*Fred Lips-
comb in "New Occasions," Jan., 1894.*

far transcends free trade in merchandise, that, having annihilated profit to capital, the continuance of the tariff would be a matter of indifference to the element that now lobbies for its continuance. What, then, would prevent its repeal?

196 So it would be with all monopolies. The competition that a surplus of capital would put in motion would checkmate and destroy them. *The exclusion of competition is as essential to monopoly as the exclusion of air is to a vacuum.* The admission of *free competition is as destructive to monopoly* as the *free admission of air is to a vacuum.* It is to monopoly that we are indebted for the corruption that has insinuated itself into and permeates the social fabric from end to end and from its center to its edges. Corruption that stultifies the intellect; that warps the judgment; that stimulates and rewards crime; that freezes the fraternal feeling; that starves love and nourishes prostitution; that has no prizes for intellect unless it can be McKinleyized or Clevelandized to serve party purposes or society fads. Its rewards and its punishments are alike its weapons of defense and its hopes of perpetuity. Under the Mutual Credit System, the tables will be turned. Corruption, no longer sustained by ill-gotten wealth, must disappear; and under the influence of the progress that a real civilization and perpetual prosperity will inaugurate, will come "the new time" of which the editor of the *Arena* so eloquently speaks, "while amazed history, gazing long before she writes, at last shall pen the story of the first civilization of earth great and wise enough to be just."

197   Both "measure of value" and "standard of value" are
terms that need a champion to save them from being blotted
from the vocabulary.

198   Measure of value!   Why not a measure of feeling,
of pain?   Really, this theme needs synthesizing!

199   The oscillations of a pendulum under the same conditions as to height from the level of the sea, temperature,
length of pendulum, stillness of the air, etc., will travel the
same distance between strokes in any part of the earth.   By
this means we obtain a fixed, definite length through an
unvarying natural law.   A unit of length is thus a possibility, but a unit of value is an impossibility.   Value, like pain
or pleasure, is not a mathematical quantity.   It has no existence except as a relation between two or more objects; a
relation which is purely metaphysical and therefore cannot
be measured.   We can only express more or less of it by
means of a conventional monetary unit,* not by a unit of

---

* "Money of account performs the same office, with regard to the
value of things, that degrees, minutes, seconds, etc., do with regard
to angles, or as scales do to geographical maps, or to plans of any
kind.   In all these inventions there is some denominative taken for
the unit.   .   .   .   Just so, the unit in money can have no invariable
determinate proportion to any part of value; that is to say, it cannot
be fixed in perpetuity to any particular quantity of gold and silver, or
any other commodity.   The value of commodities depending upon
circumstances relative to themselves, their value ought to be considered as changing with respect to one another only; consequently,
anything which troubles or perplexes the ascertaining these changes
of proportion by means of a general determinate and invariable scale,
must be hurtful to trade; and this is the infallible consequence of
every rise in the price of money or coin.   Money, as has been said,
is an ideal scale of equal parts.   If it be demanded what ought to be
the standard value of one part, I answer by putting another question:
What is the standard length of a degree, a minute, or a second?
None: and there is no necessity for any other than what, by conven-
tion, mankind think fit to give."—*Sir J. Stewart.*

itself as we express length by a unit of length, or weight by a unit of weight. As we cannot reach it by mathematics, we cannot make a unit to measure it with. It is clear, then, that we do not measure value at all. One does not say to a builder, "will you measure the cost of such a building for me?" No; we say: "Will you estimate the cost of such a building?" Does he measure the value of the building when he tells you how many dollars it will cost? No. He expresses the value in terms of money. Does your grocer or your tailor or your dry goods merchant measure values when he tells you the price of goods? How absurd! As well might we talk of measuring the number of bricks that enter into the construction of a building, or of calculating the color of a spectral ray. Value is not determined by measuring it, but by demand and supply. Whatever monopoly exists, of course affects the supply, and consequently the market value; but demand and supply, with or without monopoly, determines value; and the only proper function of money is to facilitate the distribution of things that have value, by exchanging them for it; the one who gets the money exchanging it again for something else. Now, it must be evident to anyone who will closely examine these operations, that in order that the certificates of credit (174) may pass, be accepted at their face value for the things of value, it is only necessary that they be secured credit (9, 10, 12). It is not necessary that provision be made for their redemption in a stated definite quantity of some special commodity, but that they be redeemed in anything for not less than their face value, and at the market or prevailing value or price. And this is one of the great advantages that the Mutual Credit System has over all others; its money is redeemable in all commodities at their market value instead of a single commodity in definite quantity, as is the case with "standard" money. The purchasing power of "standard" money is affected by the rise or fall in the market value of the "standard" commodity (200, 242); hence this purchasing power must vary.   Prices or market values are affected, therefore, not only by the effect of the demand and supply of the commodities themselves, but also by the variations in the purchasing power of the money.   In other words, the fluctuations in values are complex, but they will be reduced to simple fluctuations by the adoption of mutual credit money in place of "standard" money; for the exchangeable value* of the former can have no effect whatever on the market value of any commodity.   It is not a commodity, nor is it affected by any commodity.   It is simply secured or certified credit used as a means of exchanging commodities.

200   The following will, perhaps, more clearly impress this point upon the mind of the reader.   We will suppose that the Mutual Credit System has been put in operation and that both kinds of money are now in circulation.   The "standard" money is redeemable in coin; the mutual credit money is redeemable as provided in the plan† and is accepted at its face value in exchange for commodities, prices being the same as for coin money.   We will now suppose that the Mutual Credit System comes rapidly into public favor and its money is being issued in a large number of cities.   The demand for the "precious" metals to serve as a basis for money under such circumstances will very materially diminish.   What will be the effect on the market value of those metals?   They will also very naturally depreciate.   What effect will such depreciation have upon the purchasing power of the coin made of those metals?   Their purchasing power will inevitably follow the decline in the market value of the metals (242).   What effect will this decline in the market value of the "precious" metals have on the exchangeable value of the money of the Mutual Credit Association?   None whatever.   Prices, then, for such money will remain the

---

* I deprecate the use of the term "purchasing power" when applied to money that circulates on its merits.   It has acquired a meaning in connection with legal tender money and authority that disqualifies it for expressing the exchangeability of certificates of credit (359).

† See prospectus.

same; while for the first time, perhaps, in history, we shall see gold prices quoted higher than prices for its old rival,—paper money not based on gold (65), to say nothing of silver. Of course, the "standard" paper money will go down along with the coin. This is the inevitable result.

201 Now, let us examine the position of my opponents on this question of a measure or standard of value.*

202 The terms, "measure of value" and "standard of value," are used in the same sense by those who maintain their existence or necessity; they are interchangeable, so that either term may be used.

203 The supporters of the idea of a "standard of value" maintain that paper money, unless it is redeemable in a definite quantity of some special commodity, would have no definite exchangeable value; that this quantity in which the paper dollar must be redeemable, is thus constituted the "measure" and "standard" of value.† This is precisely the

---

* "Although standard and value, or definite invariable fact and indefinite variable state of mind, are as opposite as the poles, yet because we can unite the words, standard and value, into the glib phrase, "standard of value," we imagine when we have done so that fact and sentiment have thereby become welded into a reality, definite and comprehensive enough to test or measure all other things, or that we really have a "standard of value." But blinded by custom, misled by authority, and confounding exchangeability with standard of value, we cannot see that though we have a name we have not a fact, and that standard of value is an impossibility, a will-o'-the-wisp luring to ruin. Exchangeability, however great, can never be transmuted into a standard of value any more than an opinion into a fact."—*Standard of Value, by Lewis H. Blair.*

† "The argument showing impossibility of a standard of value has so far been mainly theory. The fact of the impossibility is shown by the violent antagonism of silverites and goldites, each school taking the same data, and one school proving that silver has remained stationary and gold has advanced, and the other school proving that gold has remained stationary and silver has declined, and agreement is impossible because the contention is not about something having fixed, uniform and demonstrable qualities, but about a sentiment, an opinion, a state of mind varying with time, place, individual and circumstances. Better attempt a standard of beauty or of taste or of religion, than a permanent standard of value. If we permitted ourselves to think, we would soon perceive that we are attempting sunbeams from cucumbers, and that our search was more hopeless than the quest of the Holy Grail, and quite as hopeless as the search for

position of the gold standardites, and there is no possible
escape from the same evils that result under their system of
money if we are only to change the "standard." But for-
tunately we shall be able to escape these evils, as there is no
necessity for this method of redemption being employed.
Most people are familiar with the storekeeper's money,
"good for one dollar at my store"; "good for fifty cents at
my store"; "good for twenty-five cents at my store." This
money (3-4) was not redeemable in a definite quantity of
any special commodity. It is true this money circulated only
in the immediate neighborhood of the issuer, but that was
because it was unsecured credit (9). The paper money proposed by The New Philosophy of Money will be secured
credit, and it must be admitted the one bears no comparison
to the other on that score. The point of similarity is that
neither promise a *definite quantity* of any commodity in
exchange, but so many monetary units or fractions thereof of
any commodity, in the one case, that the storekeeper had for
sale, and in the other, that any of the borrowers of the
Mutual Credit Associations have for sale. Who ever heard
of anyone refusing to take a storekeeper's promise to pay in
goods, on the ground that it did not state a definite quantity
of any particular commodity that it would be redeemed in?
The only objection ever raised against such paper money
was its unreliability. It was unsecured credit. The mutual
plan remedies this difficulty by the issue of *secured credit* in
the form of paper money, to circulate in its place. The
storekeeper's promise to pay, or anybody's promise to pay,
together with the security required, is deposited for safe
keeping until it matures. If he fails to pay his note, the
security is sold. In either case, an equal amount of the same

---

the Fountain of Youth. But because we follow in the beaten track,
we still pursue with heat and passion not only one impossibility,
namely, a single standard, but a twofold impossibility, namely, a
double standard of value—a comedy with the world for a stage, with
statesmen for actors, and the fun at the expense of the people."—
Standard of Value, by Lewis H. Blair.

paper money must come into the possession of the association that furnished it, by which act it is redeemed and retired from circulation. This method of redemption is not only as effectual as redemption by the "standard," but it is practically applicable to every dollar, while the other is not; and it is this absolute and unavoidable redemption; redemption from which there can be no possible escape, that will make its acceptance much more desirable than the other.

204   But let us still further consider the difference between redemption by the "standard of value" plan and by the Mutual Credit plan.

205   In order to redeem under the "standard" plan, it is necessary to have a sufficient amount (?) of the one thing that is said to constitute the "standard." Under the Mutual Credit plan a sufficient amount of anything that has market value will answer the purpose.

206   Under the former plan it is necessary to acquire and store a vast amount of one particular commodity. Either the amount must be equal to the total volume of paper money, in which case the volume of money must be limited to the quantity of that commodity that is obtainable, or the risk must be incurred that the demand for it to redeem with will be greater than the quantity on hand. Under the latter plan there is no need of acquiring and storing anything. Each individual takes care to pay his note when it becomes due. If he has the money it is because, after paying it out, he has taken it back again in exchange for something which he sold. This act of taking back the money which he borrowed of the Mutual Credit Association, and which he had previously paid out, is the act of redemption (244). To get it he had to give market value for it. If he has not the money, then he must get it by giving market value for it, for he must pay his note; and in paying his note the money goes back again to the association.

207   Now, what I want to impress upon the mind of the reader is the fact that, since this borrower of the Mutual

Credit Association redeems at its face value the paper money it furnished him, it is no less effectual redemption because done with some other than the special "standard" commodity. He must give full market value for it.   If, then, all the paper money issued by the association must be redeemed every twelve months in the same way, why is it not a vastly superior method of redemption to that of the gold or any other "standard" method?

208   Is the fact that within twelve months a paper dollar that is in circulation is to be retired—withdrawn from circulation—by some party who, instead of issuing it—paying it out again, returns it to the association in payment of his note that has become due—is this fact sufficient to make it acceptable money?   Can there be any possible risk in taking it?

209   As between the two, which money is the safest—that which has one chance in several in being redeemed, or that in which provision is made for the redemption of every bill within twelve months of its issue?   In the one case, the paper money is never redeemed except when an individual takes a notion to demand the "standard" for it.   In the other, it is all redeemed every twelve months without anyone bothering himself to go and demand something for which he has no use.

210   Finally, let us come to the real issue in this question of a "measure of value."   The misapprehension and confusion that befogs the minds of those who insist on the "standard of value" idea, is the result of not viewing money and the denominator, "dollar," separate and distinct from each other.*

---

* "*In other words, the coin which represents the franc, the dollar, the pound, is an entirely different thing from the franc itself, or the pound or the dollar.*   In the discussion of the financial question one of the greatest stumbling blocks in the way of a clear understanding of the matter is the fact that the coin which represents the dollar and which in common phrase is called a 'dollar' is confounded with the dollar itself. . . .   One of the most apt illustrations of this idea is that given by John Stuart Mill when he tells about the African tribes who calculate (express) the value of things by the term 'macute.' They say such a thing is worth a 'macute,' another is worth five 'macutes,' and another ten, and so on, and yet there is no such real

Each has its independent function. The one is to aid and facilitate the distribution of wealth; the other is a means by which we can express more or less value.*

211 We ask the price of a commodity and we get the answer in dollars and cents—monetary units and subdivisions —before money enters into the transaction. It is after the price has been agreed upon that the money comes into play. There are two distinct operations—the transmission from the seller to the buyer of the idea of the value of the object, by the former expressing its price in the conventional monetary unit and its subdivisions—dollars and cents. This is one operation; the other is the act of exchange, the buyer hands to the seller paper money equal to the price of the article, in exchange for it. The dollar with which we express more or less value is a conventional term, an abstraction.† The paper dollar we use as a medium of exchange is secured credit (161). In the two operations mentioned, the latter does not figure in the first, nor the former in the second. When one only inquires the price of an article, but does not buy, it is not the paper dollar that is used to convey the answer, but the term—the abstraction we call "dollar." Secured credit is divided up into certificates of credit of all denominations and called "one dollar," "two dollars," "five dollars," and so on, to correspond with the denominator or abstract dollar, thus facilitating settlement of transactions by the transfer of this

---

thing as a 'macute,' and probably never was such a thing in existence."—*Ten Men of Money Island.*

*"Money and the yardstick have nothing in common. The yardstick is an exact, unvarying measure of length. Money is an uncertain, variable measure of varying values. The yardstick is not bartered for commodities. . . . The yardstick is a unit of length. The dollar as a "unit of value" is preposterous. Our Hamilton-Jefferson statute, founding the mint, provided a dollar as our "unit of account."—*Wm. P. St. John, president of the Mercantile National Bank of New York, in statement before Committee on Banking and Currency, December, 1894.*

†"The dollar, as simple measure of value, has, like the yard, which is a measure of length, *an ideal existence, only.* In Naples, the ducat is the measure of value; but the Neapolitans have no specific coin of that denomination."—*Wm. B. Greene's "Mutual Banking," page 47.*

secured credit instead of the transfer of objects of value (coin) or paper money based on coin only.* It is for the reader to determine in his own mind whether either of these operations can be correctly called *measuring value*. The reader will no doubt find interesting the following controversy on this subject between the editor of the *Galveston News*, the editor of *Liberty*, Mr. Wm. B. DuBois, and the writer.

HOW MUCH CAN BE LOANED.

[*From Galveston News.*]

212   Mr. Alfred B. Westrup, of Chicago, has begun the publication of a paper to advocate free banking, two numbers of which have been received. Its name is the *Auditor*, and it is published at 343 Michigan Avenue. Mr. Westrup appears to have been an attentive reader of the *News*, from which he makes liberal extracts. The *Auditor* is opposed to every species of fiatism, but holds that the owners of property have a moral right to combine and do a banking business subject only to such laws as are a protection against fraud and dishonesty. The editor of the *Auditor* endorses an arti-

---

* "But we will notice briefly an argument presented in support of the proposition that the unit of money value must possess intrinsic value. The argument is derived from assimilating the constitutional provision respecting a standard of weights and measures to that conferring the power to coin money and regulate its value. It is said there can be no uniform standard of weights without weight or a measure without length or space, and we are asked how anything can be made a uniform standard of value which has itself no value. This is a question foreign to the subject before us. The legal tender acts do not attempt to make a paper standard of value. We do not rest their validity upon the assertion that their emission is coinage or any regulation of the value of money, nor do we assert that Congress may make anything which has no value money. What we do assert is, that Congress has power to enact that the government's promise to pay money shall be, for the time being, equivalent in value to the representative of value determined by the coinage act or to multiples thereof. It is hardly correct to speak of a standard of value. The Constitution does not speak of it. It contemplates a standard for that which has gravity or extension, but value is an ideal thing. The coinage act fixes its unit as a dollar, but the gold or silver thing we call a dollar is in no sense a standard of a dollar. It is a representative of it."—*Opinion of the Supreme Court, United States Legal Tender Cases; 12 Wallace, 552-3.*

cle from the *News* on a standard of valuation, but still in some portions of his writings leaves an obscurity hanging over his position in discussing the "standard of value" and "unit of value." The point which presents itself for resolution is not covered by saying that promises of dollars are accepted on an understanding. The present understanding as to a dollar is so much gold or silver or paper which is so limited that it is sure to circulate at par with coin. If issues of paper were larger the inquiry would be considerable sharper: "what is a dollar?" for the paper dollar is practically nothing but what it guarantees. And one can not pay even 101 with 100, wherefore when bank paper is lent at any interest, however low, the interest should be payable in something else than that paper. Some paper is always lost. That should be repaid in something agreed upon. There come two men to borrow, and if one gets $1,000 on certain security, by what rule shall his neighbor get $1,200 and neither more or less on other security? The *News* has explained by having an agreed standard for valuation, and it means no more or less by a standard of value. Whenever government issues are inflated and uncertain the "understanding" of the word dollar becomes too vague for dependence to be placed on it, and in mutual banking no note-holder wants a future borrower to get the issues at a more liberal rate with regard to property pledged than the earlier borrowers have got and used them at, for that would mean depreciation. Such a result is to be prevented by agreeing upon a standard for valuation, and let not this be confused with means of payment. The means of payment are the note itself and what it will bring, but there must be some thing or things uniformly referred to in determining how much shall be loaned. To refer to the bank-notes themselves might lead to limitless inflation and a very variable relation between the expanding sum of notes and the comparatively fixed sum of real things, which relation would in a while cause two or more notes to go in exchange where one had gone before, giving those who hold any money to see that by holding it they had lost purchasing power. The *Auditor* should not fear to adhere to a material standard, simple or complex, for uniform valuations and still insist upon utmost extension of the representative medium or media.

213 There seems to have been an unaccountable tendency to overlook the fact that in the system I advocate, provision

is made for the redemption of every dollar of money issued, at its face value, in commodities at their market value; and that this fact will insure its circulation, because it establishes its exchangeable value. In answer to the foregoing article, I called the attention of the *News* to the following extract from "The Financial Problem," which I reproduced in the *Auditor.*

214 "Let us suppose a community where there is only one bank, and that each individual in that community secures an account current by depositing collateral to a greater or less extent with the bank. Is it not clear that in such a system of payments, no money would be needed, every individual would pay by check; the accounts being adjusted by off-setting on the books of the bank; the *monetary unit* we call "dollar" answering the purpose of a conventional denominator or denominant. We will also suppose that this bank is conducted on the mutual plan, and therefore charges are made to cover cost only. Gold and silver bullion, like any suitable commodity, could be used as collateral, but no coin would be necessary and none would be used. It would therefore seem to be sufficiently clear that a unit to act as a measure or standard of value is but a fiction, a fetish. It is admitted that the proposed bank, for various reasons, would be an impracticable method of effecting exchanges, but the absence of a coin-unit-measure-standard would not be one of them. Not every one can have a bank account. The inconvenience of paying small amounts by checks as well as the uncertainty in many instances, as to the acceptability of checks at the bank are insurmountable difficulties, but one can hardly contemplate the foregoing and at the same time conceive how the advocates of a coin basis to paper money would defend their theory of its necessity. It is not difficult to comprehend the nature of the error here fallen into.

215 "A monetary unit (a conventional denominator or denominant) to facilitate the expressing of amounts in the realm of value, is, apparently, so similar in its function to that of the units employed in physics, such as the inch, the pound, etc., especially as certain coin is made legal tender, that the notion has become well nigh universal that this monetary unit must be a definite quantity of some commodity just as the inch is a definite and unvarying length, or the

pound is a definite and unvarying weight; but this notion is
utterly devoid of reason.*

216 "As there is nothing definite or permanent in value
a unit of value is a physical impossibility.

217 "The monetary unit is as near a unit or measure of
value as the "x" in an algebraic equation is a known quantity. You can ascertain the exchangeable value of a gold
dollar in any commodity by inquiring the price of that commodity; so also you can find the quantity "x" by ciphering
out the equation.

218 "The value of the gold dollar varies with every
change in market price, just as the quantity "x" differs with
every change in the equation.

219 "The gold dollar is a certain quantity of gold. It is
not the gold, however, but the value of the gold that is supposed to do the measuring, and it is the value of the gold that
is the uncertain quantity.

220 "How can an uncertain quantity be a unit of measure? And if it is not a measure, what is the object of a coin
basis? If it is answered that it is not a measure but a "standard" of value, if by "standard" is meant denominant, then
the use of the term "standard" is equivocal, and therefore
sophistical or dishonest. If it is claimed that it is more than
a denominant, there is no escaping the dilemma that con-
fronts the paragram "measure."

221 "When paper money is issued as proposed by the
Mutual Bank Propaganda, with ample security but not legal
tender nor redeemable in any special commodity, the monetary unit dollar will simply be a denominant. Its purchasing
power will not be affected by a rise or fall in the price of any
commodity any more than an order for a pound of butter
commands more than a pound at one time and less at another.
The mutual bank paper dollar will buy more butter at one
time than another, but this will take place in consequence of
the operation of supply and demand in regard to butter only;
and so with regard to all other commodities; the mutual
bank paper money will have no more effect on the price of
commodities than the order for the butter will affect the price
of butter (358-359), whereas when the monetary unit is a
legal tender commodity dollar, variations in the price of any
commodity are affected, not only by supply and demand in

---

* See foot-note page 94.

that particular commodity, but also "supply and demand" in the arbitrarily limited legal-tender-commodity-dollar, which limit enables a class to own and control it, the scarcity or abundance of which (dependent upon combinations among this class) must affect the price of all other commodities. Under any system, therefore, which recognizes any special commodity as a legal tender basis for its paper money, especially as that commodity must necessarily be one that is limited by nature, fluctuations in prices become complicated by complex causes, resulting from the limitations to credit through this control of money. No such effect can occur under the Mutual Credit System, the volume of money being unlimited except by the quantity of collateral offered, and the rate of interest being the same to all borrowers."

THE STANDARD OF VALUE.

To the Editor of the Auditor:

222 I have given considerable thought to the money question, and here are my conclusions in regard to the "dollar" and the much discussed "standard of value." The dollar is, or should be under a just and scientific monetary system, merely an abstract idea. No one commodity can be made an absolute unchanging standard by which to effect exchanges of other commodities, for the reason that, owing to fluctuations in supply and demand, there is no one commodity of which a given quantity and quality will always exchange for the same quantity and quality of any other commodity.

223 The scientific basis for money is labor, and its only honest use consists in exchanging the products or results of labor. Labor, therefore, is the nearest approach to a "standard," but it is not a fixed one, for the reason that even labor varies in supply and demand, in application and in results.

224 It is not necessary to have a fixed or even an approximate standard of value; it is only necessary to have a unit. In our country the dollar is that unit. But for the sake of example let us use the algebraic symbol x, and see how it works itself out in the regulation of prices. Let us bear in mind, in the first place, that the real cost of a thing is the labor it takes to produce that thing. Then, we will assume that the aver-

age daily wages of labor is 2x, and that it costs on the average to produce to the consumer:

	Days Labor
1 bushel of wheat,	½
1 barrel potatoes,	1
1 barrel flour,	2
1 pair boots,	3
1 suit of clothes,	10
1 horse,	50
1 piano,	100
1 locomotive,	1,000

The prices of these various articles will then be as follows:

1 bushel of wheat,	1x
1 barrel potatoes,	2x
1 barrel flour,	4x
1 pair boots,	6x
1 suit of clothes,	20x
1 horse,	100x
1 piano,	200x
1 locomotive,	2,000x

And these prices will vary according as the average daily wages of labor varies and according to supply and demand. It seems to me that this is the root of the whole matter and all there is to the "standard of value."

WM. B. DuBois.

Bayonne, N. J., August 14, 1891.

A STANDARD OF VALUE A NECESSITY.

[*Liberty, June 13, 1891.*]

225   Readers of *Liberty* will remember an article in number 184 on "The Functions of Money," reprinted from the *Galveston News.* In a letter to the *News* I commented upon this article as follows: "I entirely sympathize with your disposal of the *Evening Post's* attempt to belittle the function of money as a medium of exchange; but do you go far enough when you content yourself with saying that a standard of value is highly desirable? Is it not absolutely necessary? Is money possible without it? If no standard is definitely adopted, and then if paper money is issued, does not the first commodity that the first note is exchanged for

immediately become a standard of value? Is not the second
holder of the note governed in making his next purchase by
what he parted with in his previous sale? Of course it is a
very poor standard that is thus arrived at, and one that must
come in conflict with other standards adopted in the same
indefinite way by other exchanges occurring independently
but almost simultaneously with the first one above supposed.
But so do gold and silver come in conflict now. Doesn't it
all show that the idea of a standard is inseparable from
money? Moreover, there is no danger in a standard. The
whole trouble disappears with the abolition of the basis
privilege."

226   The *News* printed my letter and made the following
rejoinder: "It will occur that in emphasizing one argument
there is such need of passing others by with seeming uncon-
cern that to some minds other truths seem slighted,—truths
which also need emphasizing perhaps in an equal, or it may
be, for useful practical reasons, in a superior degree. The
News aims at illustrating one thing at a time, but it is both
receptive and grateful to those correspondents who intelligently extend its work and indicate useful subjects for discussion, giving their best thought thereon. A Boston reader,
speaking of the standard of value, states an undeniable truth
to the effect that without a thing or things of value to which
paper money can be referred and which can ultimately be
got for it, such money would be untrustworthy or worthless.
The *News* in a past article was discussing primary commerce and the transition to indirect exchange. No agreed
standard for valuation is needed while mere barter is the rule;
but it is indispensable as soon as circulating notes are issued.

227   "The vice of the greenback theory is that the notes
do not call for anything in particular, and so, if their volume
be doubled, their purchasing power must apparently decline
one-half. A note properly based on gold, silver, wheat, cotton, or other commodity has a tangible security behind it.
The one thing may be better than the other, but the principle is there in all. It is, however, a notable truth that the
standard of valuation can be nothing better than an empirical
one. Like mathematical quantities, value has no independent existence, but, unlike mathematical quantities, value has
not even existence as a quality of one object. It cannot be
compared to a measure of length, which possesses the quality
of extension in itself. Gold is assumed to vary little in rela-

tion to other things, and they to vary much in relation to gold Nobody can know how much gold does vary in the relation. The notable steadiness is in the amount of labor which will produce a given quantity and the length of time which it will last. The basis of the assumed steadiness of gold is thus found. But if the standard for use in making valuations be confessedly empirical and value an elusive quality not of things separately, but of things in relation, there is a countervailing difference between a standard of length and a standard of value, which results in disposing of the objection that the standard is empirical. Why would it be a serious objection to a yardstick if it were longer or shorter from day to day? Because thus the customer would get more or less cloth than was intended. But why is that? Because the function of the yardstick is to measure for delivery as great a length of cloth as its own length. But now let us visit a bank or insurance office. We want a loan of circulating notes or a policy of insurance. The property offered as security is valued. Assume that gold is taken as the standard, and that the loan or the policy is for $600 on a valuation of $1,000. It is no matter in these cases if the standard varies, provided it does not vary to exceed the margin between the valuation and the obligation. The property pledged is merely security for the loan, or, in the case of insurance, the premium paid is a per cent of the amount insured. The margin between the valuation and the loan is established to make the loan abundantly safe. The policy is safely written through the same expedient. The empirical standard of value has a needful compensation about it which the yardstick or other measure neither has nor needs,— namely, the valuing goods does not deliver them. It is provisional. In case of default in paying back the loan, the goods are sold and the same money borrowed is paid back, but the residue goes to the borrower. It is therefore an efficient compensation for the lack of an invariable standard of value that the actual standard in any case is simply used as a means of estimating limits within which loans are safe. All danger is avoided by giving the borrower the familiar right in case of foreclosure. It is sometimes a fine thing to discover distinctions, but it is frequently a finer thing to discover whether or not the distinctions affect the question."

228 While not hesitating for a moment to accept the *News'* explanation that, when hinting that a standard of

value is not indispensable, it was speaking of barter only, I may point out nevertheless that there was a slip of the pen, and that the words actually used conveyed the idea that something more than barter was in view.   Let me quote from the original article:

229   "It is manifest that a medium of exchange is absolutely necessary to all trade beyond barter.   A standard of value is highly desirable, but perhaps this is as much as can be safely asserted on that question."

230   It seems to me a fair interpretation of this language to claim the meaning that in *trade beyond barter* it is not sure that a standard of value is absolutely necessary.   And this interpretation receives additional justification when it is remembered that the words were used in answer to the *Evening Post's* contention that, in comparing the two functions of money, its office of medium of exchange must be held inferior to its office of measuring values.

231   However, the *News* now makes it sufficiently clear that a standard of value is absolutely essential to money, thereby taking common ground with me against the position of comrade Westrup.   Still I cannot quite agree to all that it says in comment upon the Westrup view.

232   First, I question its admission that a measure of value differs from a measure of length in that the former is empirical.   True, value is a relation; but then, what is extension? Is not that a relation also,—the relation of an object to space? If so, then the yardstick does not possess the quality of extension in itself, being as dependent for it upon space as gold is dependent for its value upon other commodities.   But this is metaphysical and may lead us far; therefore I do not insist, and pass on to a more important consideration.

233   Second, I question whether the *News'* "countervailing difference between a standard of length and a standard of value" establishes all that it claims.   In the supposed case of a bank loan secured by mortgage, the margin between the valuation and the obligation practically secures the noteholder against loss from a decline in the value of the security, but it does not secure him against loss from a decline in the value of the standard, or make it impossible for him to profit by a rise in the value of the standard.   Suppose that a farmer, having a farm worth $5,000 in gold, mortgages it to a bank as security for a loan of $2,500 in notes newly issued by the bank against this farm.   With these notes he pur-

chases implements from a manufacturer. When the mortgage expires a year later, the borrower fails to lift it. Meanwhile gold has declined in value. The farm is sold under the hammer, and brings, instead of $5,000 in gold, $6,000 in gold. Of this sum, $2,500 is used to meet the notes held by the manufacturer who took them a year before in payment for the implements sold to the farmer. Now, can the manufacturer buy back his implements with $2,500 in gold? Manifestly not, for by the hypothesis gold has gone down. Why, then, is not this manufacturer a sufferer from the varition in the standard of value, precisely as the man who buys cloth with a short yardstick and sells it with a long one is a sufferer from the variation in the standard of length? The claim that a standard of value varies, and inflicts damage by its variations, is perfectly sound; but the same is true, not only of the standard of value, but of every valuable commodity as well. Even if there were no standard of value and therefore no money, still nothing could prevent a partial failure of the wheat crop from enhancing the value of every bushel of wheat. Such evils, so far as they arise from natural causes, are in the nature of inevitable disasters and must be borne. But they are of no force whatever as an argument against the adoption of a standard of value. If every yardstick in existence, instead of constantly remaining thirty-six inches long, were to vary from day to day within the limits of thirty-five and thirty-seven inches, we should still be better off than with no yardstick at all. But it would be no more foolish to abolish the yardstick because of such a defect than it would be to abolish the standard of value, and therefore money, simply because no commodity can be found for a standard which is not subject to the law of supply and demand.

A NECESSITY OR A DELUSION,—WHICH?

[*Liberty, June 27, 1891.*]

To the Editor of Liberty:

234 It is not only a delusion, but a misuse of language, to talk of a "standard of value." Give us a standard of pain or pleasure, and you may convince us that there can be a "standard of value." I am well aware of the difficulty of

discussing this question, even with so precise an editor as
Mr. Tucker; but since he has called in question the views
presented in my pamphlet (The Financial Problem), I feel
called upon to lay before the readers of *Liberty* some additional arguments to show the correctness of what Mr. Tucker
has honored me by calling "the Westrup view."

235 Let us consider for a moment the practical workings
of a mutual bank, as near as we can foretell them.   The
incentive to organize a mutual bank is the opportunity of
borrowing money at a very low rate of interest and no additional expense.   This desideratum is not confined to a few
individuals, but is well nigh universal. It follows, therefore,
that the starting of a bank will draw to it a large number of
people, embracing producers and dealers in almost, perhaps
all, commodities. One of the conditions in obtaining the
notes (paper money) of the mutual bank is that they will be
taken in lieu of current money without variation in the price
of the commodities, by those who borrow them. This condition is just, and will be readily acquiesced in without a
murmur. At the very outset of the mutual bank, then, we
have at least dealers in most of the ordinary commodities who
will accept this money. This certainty of its redemption in
commodities at their market price in current money guarantees its circulation.

236 Strictly speaking, the mutual bank does not issue the
money; it simply furnishes it and is the custodian of the collateral pledged to insure its return. It is the borrowers who
both issue and redeem.

237 The transaction between the bank and the borrower
is of no interest to the public previous to the *issue* of any of
the money by the borrower. Neither is it concerned with
the transaction between the borrower and the bank after the
former has redeemed all the money he borrowed.

238 Discussing theories is far less important than efforts
to put in practice such momentous reforms as the application
of the mutual feature to the supply of the medium of exchange. If comrade Tucker really desires the establishment
of mutual banks, it seems to me he would naturally discuss
the practicability of such institutions. Let him point out
wherein the above forecast is unsound. Let him show the
necessity for a "standard of value" and suggest how to intro-
duce one; perhaps I may become converted. I shall most
surely acknowledge my error if I am convinced, but I have

no time or inclination to discuss any abstract theory about a "standard of value." The one question that seems to me of importance is the practicability of the mutual bank. If it is not practicable, why is it not so? If it is, why waste time and space in discussing whether the first or the second or any other commodity exchanged becomes the "measure" or "standard" of value; especially as "the whole trouble disappears with the abolition of the basis privilege "

ALFRED B. WESTRUP.

239 Mr. Westrup's article sustains in the clearest manner my contention that money is impossible without a standard of value. Starting out to show that such a standard is a delusion, he does not succeed in writing four sentences descriptive of his proposed bank before he adopts that "delusion." He tells us that "one of the conditions in obtaining the notes (paper money) of the mutual bank is that they will be taken *in lieu of current money*." What does this mean? Why, simply that the patrons of the bank agree to take its notes as the equivalent of gold coin of the same face value. In other words, they agree to adopt gold as a standard of value. They will part with as much property in return for the notes as they would part with in return for gold. And if there were no such standard, the notes would not pass at all, because nobody would have any idea of the amount of property that he ought to exchange for them. The *naïveté* with which Mr. Westrup gives away his case shows triumphantly the puerility of his raillery at the idea of a standard of value.

240 Indeed, comrade Westrup, I ask nothing better than to discuss the practicability of mutual banks. All the work that I have been doing for liberty these nineteen years has been directed steadily to the establishment of the conditions that alone will make them practicable. I have no occasion to show the necessity for a standard of value. Such necessity is already recognized by the people whom we are trying to convince of the truth of mutual banking. It is for you, who deny this necessity, to give your reasons. And in the very moment in which you undertake to tell us why you deny it, you admit it without knowing it. It would never have occurred to me to discuss the abstract theory of a standard of value. I regard it as too well settled. But when you, one of the most conspicuous and faithful apostles of mutual bank-

8

ing, begin to bring the theory into discredit and ridicule by
basing your arguments in its favor on a childish attack
against one of the simplest of financial truths, I am as much
bound to repudiate your heresy as an engineer would be to
disavow the calculations of a man who should begin an
attempt to solve a difficult problem in engineering by denying the multiplication table.

241   I fully recognize Mr. Westrup's faithful work for
freedom in finance and the ability with which he often
defends it.   In fact, it is my appreciation of him that has
prevented me from criticising his error earlier.   I did not
wish to throw any obstacle in the path or in any way
dampen the enthusiasm of this ardent propagandist.   But
when I see that admirable paper, *Egoism*, of San Francisco,
putting forward those writings of Mr. Westrup which contain the objectionable heresy; and when I see that other
admirable paper, *The Herald of Anarchy*, of London, led
by his or similar ideas to advocate the issue of paper bearing
on its face the natural prices of all commodities (!); and
when I see individualists holding Anarchism responsible for
these absurdities and on the strength of them making effective attacks upon a financial theory which, when properly
defended, is invulnerable,—it seems high time to declare that
the free and mutual banking advocated by Proudhon, Greene,
and Spooner never contemplated for a moment the desirabil-
ity or the possibility of dispensing with a standard of value.
If others think that a standard of value is a delusion, let
them say so by all means; but let them not say so in the
name of the financial theories and projects which the original
advocates of mutual banking gave to the world.

242   I have endeavored all through this lengthy contention for what is sound and logical in regard to the exchangeability of paper money, to be fair in presenting the position
of those who differ from me on this question; and that the
reader may be able to judge impartially as to the correct view,
I have reproduced entire articles, instead of extracts.   Mr.
Tucker replies to my statement (203) namely, that mutual
money will circulate freely because borrowers bind themselves
to take it in exchange for commodities, the same as they do

current money, "that the patrons of the bank agree to take
its notes as the equivalent of gold coin of the same face value.
In other words, they agree to adopt gold as a standard of
value." But how does he reconcile his theory with the fact
admitted in his controversy with Mr. Fisher? ("Instead of
a Book," page 233.) "The value of gold would be reduced
by mutual banking, because it would thereby be stripped of
that exclusive monetary utility conferred upon it by the State
(199-200). The percentage of this reduction, no one can
tell in advance." And how does he reconcile the above with
the following which he quotes from Col. Greene? "MUT-
UAL MONEY IS MEASURED BY SPECIE, BUT IS IN NO WAY
ASSIMILATED TO IT; AND THEREFORE, ITS ISSUE CAN
HAVE NO EFFECT WHATEVER TO CAUSE A RISE OR FALL
IN THE PRICE OF THE PRECIOUS METALS." He not only
quotes it approvingly, but says: "This is one of the most
important truths in finance" (Ibid, 232). Here we have
two statements which are as opposed to each other as are the
pages on which they are printed. "The value of gold would
be reduced by mutual banking. . . . . its issue (mutual
money) can have no effect whatever to cause a rise or fall in
the price of the precious metals." Of course Mr. Tucker is
right in the first statement, and both he and Col. Greene are
therefore necessarily wrong in the second statement. "Mutual money is measured by specie!" If this is true, then
mutual money must follow the decline in the value of gold
which will follow its issue. The issue of mutual money
then, will cause a rise in prices, because it will cause a depreciation of the value of gold. Mutual money being "measured by specie" will go down with the gold, and consequently will also be reduced in exchangeable value, which is
the same thing as a rise in other values. To what confusion
of thought does the infatuation over an idea lead! If mutual
money is to be measured by specie, we are indeed in a bad
fix, and all the evils predicted by our opponents will surely
come to pass if the Mutual Credit System is established.

243   But there is no danger that the evils will occur.
Mutual money will not be "measured by specie," nor will
any one part with it for less than its face value.   There will
be a reason for depreciation in gold.   It will be "deprived of
that exclusive monetary utility conferred upon it by the
State"—the making it legal tender: but there will be no reason for depreciation in mutual money, because the demand
for it to pay notes of borrowers which have become due at
the Mutual Credit Association will always be in exact ratio
to the volume in circulation.   In other words, the demand
for the certificates of credit, in order to retire them from circulation by payment of notes to the Mutual Credit Association will be as constant as their issue; hence, this money will
be more acceptable, as currency, than anything that can
compete with it.   For this reason, it will not depreciate or
follow the downward course of gold.   Gold will go out of
use as money and mutual money will take its place.

244   Mr. Tucker fails to comprehend the true nature of
exchange or of value, when he says: "Mr. Westrups article
sustains in the clearest manner my contention that money is
impossible without a standard of value.   Starting out to
show that such a standard is a delusion, he does not succeed
in writing four sentences descriptive of his proposed bank,
before he adopts that 'delusion'."   I did not start out to show
that "such a standard" is a delusion, but that "standard of
value" is not a concept but a delusion.   Mr. Tucker's contention is "that money is impossible without a standard of
value."   I claim, and have never given cause for any one to
think I meant otherwise, that paper money is impossible (so
long as all are not perfectly honest) unless its redemption is
satisfactorily provided for.   Mr. Tucker says that the only
satisfactory provision is a definite quantity of some special
commodity obtainable on demand in exchange for the paper
money, and that this quantity is the "standard of value."
This is the position of the professors and the "great financiers," and as I have previously stated, there is no escaping

the evils resulting from cornering the "standard" and then
demanding it in redemption of the paper money, which can
be done by a class interested in depreciating the paper
money purely for speculative purposes, no matter what commodity be selected as the "standard." And I claim that a
quantity of any commodity cannot be a standard of value,
because the value of that quantity is not fixed but is ever
subject to change; that to call that which is changeable, a
standard, is to talk nonsense; that the redemption provided
by the Mutual Credit system, which is to the effect that each
certificate shall be retired from circulation by rendering to
the holder its face value in commodities at their market value
or price, is an absolute guaranty of their entire acceptability
in exchange for commodities, not affecting change in values
as "standard" money does, but their abundance and low rate
of interest will promote enterprise and facilitate exchanges
on a cash basis. While Col. Greene refers to "standard of
value" as though there was such a thing, he made no provision for it in his plan for mutual banks.* I appreciate Col.
Greene's writings and acknowledge my indebtedness to him;

---

* The Mutual Credit System (see plan) is proposed as an improvement on Col. Greene's Mutual Bank, which was as follows:

1. The inhabitants, or any portion of the inhabitants, of any town
or city in the Commonwealth, may organize themselves into a
Mutual Banking Company.

2. Any person may become a member of the Mutual Banking
Company of any particular town, by pledging REAL ESTATE situated
in that town, or in its immediate neighborhood, to the Mutual Bank
of that town.

3. The Mutual Bank of any town may issue *paper money* to circulate as currency among persons willing to employ it as such.

4. Every member of a Mutual Banking Company shall bind himself, and be bound in due legal form, on admission, to receive in payment of debts, at par, and from all persons, the bills issued, and to be
issued, by the particular Mutual Bank to which he may belong; but
no member shall be obliged to receive, or have in possession, bills of
said Mutual Bank to an amount exceeding the whole value of the
property pledged by him.

5. Any member may borrow the paper money of the bank to
which he belongs, on his own note running to maturity (without
indorsement), to an amount not to exceed one-half of the value of
the property pledged by him.

6. The rate of interest at which said money shall be loaned by the

but to call his pamphlet the "standard work" on the subject
sounds a little too orthodox to come from an Anarchist, especially when it contains the glaring error I have pointed out
(242), and which Mr. Tucker reproduced as "one of the
most important truths in finance."

245 Another error of Mr. Tucker's is that of naming
Spooner (241) as an advocate of free and mutual banking.
Mr. Spooner never advocated mutual banking, at all.   His
scheme is a joint-stock affair, involving interest to those who
do not "get in on the ground floor," and, of course, dividends
to those who do.   This is neither free nor mutual banking
and is on a par with Mr. Hugo Bilgram's proposition in his
recent book, "A Study of the Money Question," which advocates free banking, but nevertheless presents a plan for a system of money to be run by the government and in which
poor borrowers who cannot muster up enough security to
borrow $1,000 are to be ignored and left to the mercy of
money sharks.   When I invited Mr. Tucker to "show the
necessity for a standard of value" and suggest how to intro-
duce one, he declined, saying, "I have no occasion to show
the necessity for a standard of value.   Such necessity is
already recognized by the people whom we are trying to
convince of the truth of mutual banking."   This would seem
to imply that since the people believe in it, and Col. Greene

---

bank shall be determined by, and shall, if possible, just meet and
cover the bare expenses of the institution.

7. No money shall be loaned by the bank to persons who do not
become members of the company by pledging real estate to the bank.

8. Any member, by paying his debts to the Mutual Bank to
which he belongs, may have his property released from pledge, and
be himself released from all obligations to said Mutual Bank, and to
holders of the Mutual Bank money, as such.

9. No Mutual Bank shall receive other than Mutual Bank paper
money in payment of debts due it, except at a discount of one-half of
one per cent.

10. The Mutual Banks of the several counties in the Commonwealth shall be authorized to enter into such arrangements with each
other as shall enable them to receive each other's bills in payments
of debts; so that, for example, a Fitchburg man may pay his debts to
the Barre Bank in Oxford money, or in such o'her Worcester county
money as may suit his convenience.

believed in it, it is not necessary to determine whether it is an error or not. But since Col. Greene made no provision for a "standard," and since his mutual money would not have been "measured by specie," as he affirmed, because "the value of gold would be reduced by mutual banking," etc., there would have been no "standard of value" in his system any more than there is in the one I propose, which differs from his only in some features I have added. If Mr. Tucker sees the necessity for a "standard of value" in connection with mutual banking, he can make fame for himself if he will invent a method of applying it to that system. I challenge him to do it; and I further predict that when he applies his own mind to the consideration of the question instead of depending upon Col. Greene or "standard works on the subject," he will admit my position to be the correct one. I am sorry for his unreasonable opposition, because it has materially retarded the movement. As an illustration of this, let the reader turn to Mr. Tucker's letter to the *News* (225) and the *News'* rejoinder (226-227); then the comments of Mr. Tucker (228, 233). "A standard of value is highly desirable, but perhaps this is as much as can be safely asserted on that question." Unlike Mr. Tucker, the *News* is receptive to the correct view, and he was altogether too hasty in assuming that the *News* took "common ground with me (him) against the position of comrade Westrup." It says: "A note properly based on gold, silver, wheat, cotton, or other commodity, has a tangible security behind it." The "standard for valuation" which it says is indispensable as soon as circulating notes are issued" does not necessarily mean a standard of value, but the denominator "dollar."

246 Under the Mutual Credit System, value is expressed and secured credit is divided by this denominator, facilitating the exchange of equivalents of one for the other. This secured credit being based on gold, silver, wheat, cotton, or other commodities, and therefore having a "tangible security behind it," cannot depreciate, and it is for this reason and

because borrowers bind themselves to take the certificates into which it is divided and issued, at their face value in payment of debt and in exchange for commodities and services without discriminating in prices, as long as they are members of the Mutual Credit Association.   I have felt warranted in extending this chapter to so great a length because of the importance of the subject.   It is the question about which it is probable the hardest fighting will be done when free money becomes a national issue.   It is a theme on which financiers and politicians can talk glibly, and about which they will incur the least danger of being understood.

CONTROVERSY BETWEEN ALFRED B. WESTRUP AND EDWARD ATKINSON IN REGARD TO THE MUTUAL CREDIT ASSOCIATION.

The following correspondence explains itself.

MINNEAPOLIS, MINN., March 18, 1894.

EDWARD ATKINSON, Esq.,
Boston, Mass.

DEAR SIR:

As I desire to publish in permanent form my criticism of your *North American Review* article, "How Distrust Stops Trade," your reply and my rejoinder, I wish to give you an opportunity to correct or add thereto whatever you may wish to supplement. I insist on fair play. I am always willing to grant it.

Very respectfully,
ALFRED B. WESTRUP.

———

BOSTON, March 23, 1894.

ALFRED B. WESTRUP, Esq.,
Minneapolis, Minn.

DEAR SIR:

Your letter of the 18th has been received in the absence of Mr. Atkinson. He is out of town and will probably be absent about ten days.

Yours respectfully,
G. HAMILTON.

———

Up to this date (December, 1894), I have heard nothing further from Mr. Atkinson, so our statements reappear as they were originally published.

THE NEGLECTED ELEMENTS IN THE MONEY QUESTION.

*A paper read by Alfred B. Westrup at a meeting of Minneapolis
business men and published in the Minneapolis Times.*

247   The Duke of Argyll, in his recent work, "The
Unseen Foundations of Society," struck the key-note in the
discordant and unreconcilable "dismal science" called political
economy, when he showed that there are elements which the
professors are not familiar with and which, therefore, they
have neglected to consider.   But the Duke of Argyll has
allowed some elements to escape his notice, also, and is, therefore, amenable to the same charge he makes against the
political economists.   He is an advanced thinker in some
respects, yet, in common with all the popular writers, his
conservatism has defeated his reaching bottom, if such was
his purpose.

248   The preconceived notion!   How   many   men or
women can rise above it and welcome the truth; discriminate
between conflicting theories, much less penetrate into the
unknown; that no elements may be neglected, no facts overlooked?

249   It is my purpose in this paper to call the attention of
Mr. Edward Atkinson to his shortcomings in this respect;
and if I can score a point against him it will be equally
effective against Argyll and the other writers.   In his
article, "How Distrust Stops Trade," in the July, 1893,
number of the *North American Review*, he has very forcibly shown the evil effects of bad money, but if his philosophy
had included the neglected elements I shall presently bring
to his notice, he would have written a very different article.
Mr. Atkinson's argument centers upon credit and good
money.   He says:

250   *a.* "The credit which each man can extend to his
neighbor depends not only upon the quality of the man, but
also upon the quality of the money which is to be paid and

which is to be received.   When a doubt exists about the
quality of the money, trade stops."

251   *b.* "Credit cannot be given even to those who are
entitled to it when the credit of the money itself is doubtful.
That is what affects trade now.   The quality of the money
which is lawful in the United States is doubted.   Why?
Money that is doubted is bad money.   It is not fit to be used."

252   *c.* "The only definition of good money is that it consists of coin which is worth as much after it is melted into
bullion as it purported to be worth in the coin."

253   I will now point out the neglected elements, the failure to recognize, and therefore non-participation of which, in
the effort to solve the money question, has led to the errors
and almost inextricable confusion which characterizes orthodox political economy.

254   The neglected elements are: First, the necessity for
a system of secured credit; second, the possibilities of paper
money in the extension of credit; third, the right of the
individual.

255   Mr. Atkinson's statements in *a* and *b* are lamenta-
tions that leave an aching void.   "The credit which each
man can extend to his neighbor depends not only upon the
quality of the man."   Then it does depend upon the quality
of the man (this is personal credit); and it is stated as one of
the difficulties we have to contend with.   Now, what are we
to think of the pilots who, when they run up against a snag,
climb over it instead of clearing the channel that navigation
may be free from all obstructions?   "Credit cannot be given
to those who are entitled to it."   To deny a man that which
he is entitled to is an injustice—an outrage! (23, 30)   Yet
here are these pilots, leaders, teachers, whom the people rely
on as guides, acknowledging a glaring wrong of stupendous
magnitude, for which they offer no remedy, for if his "only
definition of good money" were admitted as correct and carried into effect, it could not afford relief from that which, in
the absence of secured credit is unavoidable—a resort to unse-

cured credit (93).   It is the inadequacy of our money systems that prevent us from transacting all business on a cash
basis (58).   It is imperative to adopt a system that will
admit of such a possibility—a system of secured credit that
Mr. Atkinson fails to see the necessity for (48, 95).

256   Credit is divided into two kinds—personal or unsecured, and real or secured.   To illustrate: When goods are
sold the payment of which is deferred until some future time,
and no security is pledged to make good the payment in case
of default, it is unsecured credit.

257   When goods are sold for cash, or the payment of
which is immediate and in paper money (when payment is
made in coin it is barter)(81-88), or when the payment is
guaranteed by a pledge of security, it is secured credit (79-
91).   The former (personal or unsecured credit) has no place
in a treatise on economics (95a).   It is a personal matter with
which the economist has nothing to do.   The business of the
economist is to devise a system of secured credit that would
be satisfactory, in order that we may not be compelled to
resort to unsecured credit in the exchange of commodities or
service as is unavoidable under the present money system.
It will be conceded on all sides that cash or secured credit is
preferable to unsecured credit, and it will not be disputed that
under the present money system it would be impossible to do
all business on a cash basis, time being given to receive and
examine goods only.   For any one or many to voluntarily
give personal credit to some is quite natural, but that no system of secured credit has been put into practical operation, or
has ever been suggested by the professors, is the worst
blunder that has ever been committed; and, as I have said,
shows plainly that Mr. Atkinson fails to perceive the necessity for a system of secured credit.

258   Second: Up to the present time, the moneyed interests have been so managed that the enormous advantage of
paper money, instead of having been utilized in extending
credit in the interest of the borrower, has been used as a

means of speculation in the hands of the lender. If Mr. Atkinson had not overlooked the fact that the use of paper money admits of a system whereby credit can be issued in that form on any commodity that can be safely warehoused, as well as on immovable property, he would not have dragged the character of the individual into the discussion. Given adequate security, the quality of the applicant for credit should have no more to do with his obtaining it, than his religious belief or his political creed.

259 Mr. Atkinson's "only definition of good money" is the stock argument in favor of coin money—the dogmatic assertion that only coin it money. But this position was surrendered the moment they issued paper in excess of coin on deposit. It was repudiated when issued on United States bonds, and again in the issue of clearing-house certificates.

260 *When a specie paying bank issues an excess of paper over coin, the excess is the unsecured credit of the banker.* Now, I want to know if the borrower who borrows this unsecured credit of the banker, and puts up good security, why those who take the paper money he has borrowed of the banker would not be better protected against loss if the security was pledged to secure them, instead of being turned over to the banker to secure him? Again: If clearing-houses, which are associations of bankers, can issue money called "clearing-house certificates," thus inflating the currency and enabling them to loan more money at a rate of interest that leaves them a profit, why cannot the borrowers who put up good security organize an association and issue paper money also? The paper money would be utilized in the interest of the borrower, and as already stated, a system of secured credit would be established.*

261 Third: It is a universal practice with political economists, and Mr. Atkinson is no exception, to ignore the right of the individual. They affirm a method to be correct and

---

* See Prospectus.

call upon the individual to submit to the inconveniences or
burdens it imposes, attributing them to the perversity of
human nature, instead of pursuing investigation to discover
the real cause.   Thus, when Mr. Atkinson says, "credit cannot be given even to those who are entitled to it," he con-
cedes that they are subject to conditions which others control,
the remedy for which is that such control shall cease, or in
other words, the institution of a system that others cannot
control; that under any and all circumstances, those who are
entitled to credit will be able to get it without let or hindrance.   This reasoning recognizes the right of the individual and affords him the opportunity to help himself.

262   But Mr. Atkinson contemplates nothing of the kind.
I will grant, for the sake of argument, that the bullion value
of every coin in the United States is equal to its face value.
How is the individual who wants credit and has ample security, to obtain it?   This seems too deep for Mr. Atkinson.   He
has nothing to offer.   Such individuals are turned over to the
tender mercies of the money-lenders, or to those who have
the goods he needs.   "The money which is lawful being no
longer doubted, he will be able to get all the credit which he
is entitled to."   Let us see if this is true.

263   Paper money is a form of credit.   It is the most
desirable form of credit when it is secured credit.   The
source of paper money in this country is the United States
government.   It is issued to those only who have gold, silver
and United States bonds (17-21).   The individual who has
security other than gold, silver or United States bonds, is
denied the right to this form of credit, because paper money
is not issued to him on his security, and he is therefore
dependent upon those to whom it has been issued.

264   Credit, then, in this form, is not only limited by a
political institution, but it is furnished without interest to
exceedingly few individuals, and they loan it out to all the
rest of the inhabitants who must borrow, at such high rates as
this monopoly can enforce.   This constitutes a denial of the

right of private property (30).   If one cannot use his property for purposes of credit without he obtains the consent of
another, to that extent that other controls his property.   He
cannot get credit except as he obtains the consent of another
and pays a bonus—interest in excess of cost (95).

265   This latter represents nothing but the monopoly price
of credit (95b).   This statement constitutes a refutation of
Mr. Atkinson's position.   It is not true that under the prevailing systems of money the individual can obtain the credit
he is entitled to (105).   Nor can he under any system save
the one I propose—the establishment of Mutual Credit Associations to print and furnish certificates of credit of all denominations to such individuals as can put up good security, such
borrowers to bind themselves in legal form to accept the said
certificates in payment of debt at their face value, and also in
exchange for commodities or services without discriminating
in prices.

266   Life insurance, and Mr. Atkinson knows that fire
insurance, also, has been successful on the mutual plan; why
not banking?

267   The cost of issuing this money and taking care of
the security would not exceed one per cent per annum (316).
It would necessarily result in all credit taking that form as
rapidly as possible, as any business man can see that it will be
a great saving to borrow money at that rate and pay cash
rather than buy on time credit.

268   What I propose is the establishment of a commercial
system of money instead of the existing political system.
We have outgrown the old system and we must prepare for
the new.   Evolution is as imperative in monetary affairs as it
is in all others.

---

269   September 4th, the day my criticism of Mr. Atkinson's article appeared in the *Times*, I called on Mr. John
Blanchard, the editor, and had quite a long talk with him.

He told me he would write to Mr. Atkinson asking him to reply to my criticism and would enclose a copy of the same. The following communication shows that he did so.

THE MUTUAL CREDIT SCHEME.

[*Minneapolis Times, Sept. 12, 1893.*]

To the Editor of the Times:

270   I have your letter of the 4th, and in response to your request that will write a rejoinder to A. B. Westrup's review of a certain article of my own, I beg to say that Mr. Westrup's statement of his scheme for paper money is so incomplete as to make it impossible to subject it to scientific criticism.   Before any discussion can be had upon this old and familiar conception of a Mutual Credit Association furnishing certificates of credit, it is necessary for Mr. Westrup to define the standard of redemption by which the valuation or mental estimate of the worth of these certificates is to be established.

271   Again, if I comprehend Mr. Westrup, he would give credit money an absolute quality, to the end that its acceptance by a vendor would require no consent on his part. His argument implies that a man who desires to buy commodities or services is entitled to something that he can use as a medium of exchange, which he may use without the consent of the other party in each transaction and without regard to his own personal character, standing or property.   What is the standard of redemption of that type of credit?

272   Mr. Westrup proposes to establish a Mutual Credit Association "to print and furnish certificates of credit of all denominations to such individuals as can put up good security, such borrowers to bind themselves in legal form to accept such certificates in payment of debts at their face value and also in exchange of commodities and services, without discriminating in prices."   If Mr. Westrup proposes to make such an organization, why does he not proceed to do so?   He is as free to move in the matter as others are free to refuse. It is a very old and familiar conception.   There is no objection to it provided any number of people can be persuaded to go into it.   Why do not Mr. Westrup and his coadjutors, if any, undertake this method of making exchanges?   There is nothing to hinder.

273 Now, unless Mr. Westrup can state what the standard of redemption in his proposed system is to be, then I think he must either be held to be incapable of dealing with the subject, or else business men of long experience, economists and others who have studied the monetary question are incapable of comprehending what Mr. Westrup means. In either event, it would be a waste of time for men of experience in business, or men who have made a long study of monetary science to enter into any discussion of this old and familiar fallacy. The fault with it is, that without an act of legal tender behind them such certificates will not pass; with an act of legal tender forcing them into use, they would be a fraud.

Yours very truly,

EDWARD ATKINSON.

The following is my reply to Mr. Atkinson's rejoinder.

THE MUTUAL CREDIT SCHEME.

[*Minneapolis Times, Sept. 13, 1893.*]

To the Editor of the Times:

274 In your issue of today you print a communication from Edward Atkinson, purporting to be a rejoinder to my criticism of his *North American Review* article. Reading carefully the communication, I find no reference whatever to my criticisms. His "rejoinder" is devoted entirely to the Mutual Credit Association scheme, of which he says his knowledge is "so incomplete as to make it impossible to subject it to scientific criticism."

275 I criticise him for neglecting certain elements relating to the subject he is constantly writing about, and, instead of answering my criticisms, he evades the issue by writing a third of a column in opposition to a scheme he admits he does not understand.

276 Omitting my arguments to sustain my position, because they would take up too much space, I will merely quote the charge I brought against Mr. Atkinson in the review alluded to.

277 "It is my purpose in this paper to call the attention of Edward Atkinson to his shortcomings in this respect; and

if I can score a point against him, it will be equally effective against Argyll and the other writers. In his article, "How Distrust Stops Trade," in the July, 1893, number of the *North American Review*, he has very forcibly shown the evil effects of bad money, but if his philosophy had included the neglected elements I shall presently bring to his notice, he would have written a very different article. . . . .

278 "I will now point out the neglected elements, the failure to recognize, and therefore non-participation of which, in the effort to solve the money question, has led to the errors and almost inextricable confusion which characterizes orthodox political economy.

279 "The neglected elements are: First, the necessity for a system of secured credit; second, the possibilities of paper money in the extension of credit; third, the right of the individual."

280 In answer to a letter from the editor of the *Times* enclosing my entire article asking him to respond to it, Mr. Atkinson writes: "I have your letter of the 4th, and in response to your request that I will write a rejoinder to A. B. Westrup's review of a certain article of my own, I beg to say that Mr. Westrup's statement of his scheme for paper money is so incomplete as to make it impossible to subject it to scientific criticism."

281 There is not a word in all the rest of his communication about my accusation that he has overlooked elements relating to the money question, and anyone familiar with correct methods of conducting a discussion will readily see that he has evaded the point at issue.

282 I affirm that Mr. Atkinson's philosophy ignores the rights of the individual who has security, to credit, and therefore he is ignorant of the necessity for a secured credit system, which the extension of credit by means of the invention of paper money, makes possible. Does Mr. Atkinson prove that this statement is not true by trying to show that the Mutual Credit Association plan is impracticable? It is begging the question; and I insist that he meet the issue fairly and apply his "scientific criticism" to aid the establishment of a system that recognizes and embodies these neglected elements.

283 Now, a few words about Mr. Atkinson's attempt to criticise the Mutual Credit Association plan. He says: "Mr. Westrup's statement of his scheme for paper money is

so incomplete as to make it impossible to subject it to scientific criticism"; and yet in his very next statement he says: "Before any discussion can be had on this old and familiar conception of a Mutual Credit Association furnishing certificates of credit, it is necessary for Mr. Westrup to define the standard of redemption by which the valuation or mental estimate of the worth of these certificates is to be established."

284   The public should know that Mr. Atkinson's familiarity with the mutual credit idea was derived from the author of "Mutual Banking," Col. Wm. B. Greene, with whom he debated on the subject on a public platform many years ago, and that if his knowledge of my "scheme" is incomplete, it is his fault, as in 1891 I mailed him copies of my two pamphlets and a copy of each number of my paper, the *Auditor*, as long as I published it.   I also sent him duplicate copies of a series of questions with a request that he answer them, but which answers I never received.

285   It would seem as though the following quotation which he makes from my review of his article is a satisfactory answer to his query about a "standard of redemption."

286   "Mr. Westrup proposes to establish a Mutual Credit Association 'to print and furnish certificates of credit of all denominations to such individuals as can put up good security, such borrowers to bind themselves in legal form to accept such certificates in payment of debts at their face value and also in exchange for commodities and services without discriminating in prices'."

287   It is very hard for these political economists to realize that there is no standard in value, that the monetary unit, "dollar," being conventionally agreed upon, is all that is possible to form a "mental estimate," not of their worth, but by which we can convey from one mind to another the market value of commodities.

288   It is clear that Mr. Atkinson has not yet grasped the idea of the Mutual Credit Association plan for paper money. The certificates are redeemed every time a member of the association accepts them in payment of debt or in exchange for commodities, and they are issued whenever a member pays debts or buys commodities with them.   If a member pays out some of this money and fails to take it back exchange or in payment, the association places his security— which he had to pledge to get the money—on the market, and redeems the money itself by accepting it in payment. It is then destroyed.   ALFRED B. WESTRUP.

289   It was not possible within the limits of a newspaper article to point out all the unreasonableness contained in Mr. Atkinson's rejoinder, and it is necessary to review it a little more at length.   In the second paragraph Mr. Atkinson says: "If I comprehend Mr. Westrup he would give credit money an absolute quality, to the end that its acceptance by a vendor would require no consent on his part.   His argument implies that a man who desires to buy commodities or services is entitled to something that he can use as a medium of exchange, which he may use without the consent of the other party in each transaction, and without regard to his own personal character, standing, or property."   In the very next paragraph he quotes from the proposed plan of the Mutual Credit Association what proves that the foregoing is not true.   He says: "Mr. Westrup proposes to establish a Mutual Credit Association 'to print and furnish certificates of credit of all denominations to such individuals as can put up good security, such borrowers to bind themselves in legal form to accept such certificates in payment of debt, at their face value, and also in exchange of commodities and services without discriminating in prices."   Any one who thinks must know that the paper money of an association cannot be made legal tender.   Indeed, The New Philosophy of Money is utterly opposed to legal tender money.   How, then, can the certificates of credit of the Mutual Credit Association be used to buy or pay debt "without the consent of the other party in each transaction?"   And if it is to be furnished only to "such individuals as can put up good security," why does he say, "and without regard to his own personal character, standing, or property?"   The latter part of this statement is not true. The borrower *must put up property that is good security* before he can get the certificates.   What, then, has his personal character or standing to do with it?   Continuing, within three lines of what has just been quoted, he says: "There is no objection to it provided any number of people can be persuaded to go into it."   He first concludes that the

Mutual Credit Association is a scheme to furnish "money" to anyone who needs it regardless of his "personal character, standing, or property," and which he may use "without the consent of the other party in each transaction," and yet he says, "there is no objection to it provided any number of people can be persuaded to go into it." What a travesty on common sense is this! But then, this is not "scientific criticism," the reader must remember: Mr. Atkinson can perhaps label it for him.

290 The "standard of redemption," which Mr. Atkinson lays so much stress upon, as the reader will readily understand, has reference to the definite quantity of some special commodity redemption fake, of which so much has already been said; so I will pass that by. I must, however, once more call attention to Mr. Atkinson's evasion of my criticism. I charge him with neglecting certain essential elements relating to this subject, and the charge is equally applicable to all the political economists. These elements are: the imperative necessity for a system of secured credit to take the place of the present unsecured credit system; the possibilities of paper money in the extension of credit; or, in other words, the application of the invention of paper money to the needs, and in the interest of borrowers instead of in the interest of money-lenders; and lastly the recognition of the right of the individual to use his property for purposes of credit. The present system of money is the result of efforts on the part of money-lenders and politicians to have what suited their purpose. It is the mother of interest. It enables greed to accumulate wealth it did not earn; and it perpetuates poverty and ignorance, which enables the politicians the more effectually to gratify their ambition to rule. The political economist, instead of calling attention to the neglected elements, and insisting on their recognition as principles which must not be ignored in providing a medium of exchange, have ever been lavish in apoligies, and energetic in defense of the existing system; Mr. Atkinson being one of

the most persistent. But while lack of familiarity with the
money question admits of many ambiguous statements passing
for profound wisdom, it surely is not beyond the power of
any one who can read ordinary English intelligently to perceive the glaring absurdity in the following, which is the way
Mr. Atkinson commences his letter: "I have your letter of
the 4th, and in response to your request that I will write a
rejoinder to A. B. Westrup's review of a certain article of my
own, I beg to say that Mr. Westrup's statement of his scheme
for paper money is so incomplete as to make it impossible to
subject it to scientific criticism." The eternal fitness of things,
which is here so utterly disregarded, can be more readily
understood by the following illustration: A certain individual of great fame as an astronomer writes an essay on the
philosophy of the spectral ray. Another individual who is
only an inventor of a spectroscope criticizes the eminent
astronomer, affirming that he has neglected to consider certain elementary facts; whereupon the eminent astronomer
writes a "rejoinder" stating that while he has never seen the
inventor's spectroscope, and only had a vague idea of what it
consisted, he nevertheless affirmed that it was only a delusion
and would not do the work it was claimed it would. The
eminent astronomer, not being able to meet the arguments of
his critic, contented himself by calling in question the practicability of his critic's invention; as though (admitting its
defects) it could possibly have any bearing on the correctness
of his own position. So Mr. Atkinson, failing in ability to
defend himself against the charges I make, comes back at me
with, *neither will your scheme work.* If it were admitted,
for the sake of argument, that the mutual credit idea is only
a "familiar fallacy," would it prove that in his philosophy of
money, he has not failed to take into consideration certain
factors which I call neglected elements? In his answer to
the editor of the *Times*, he says: "I have your letter of the
4th, and in response to your request that I will write a
rejoinder to A. B. Westrup's review of a certain article of my

own, . . ." He is requested to answer my criticisms of
a certain article of his. Does he do it? No; he never refers
to them at all, but goes off on another subject which was not
mentioned in the article criticized. It is just such loose reasoning as this that characterizes most of the writings of these
famous political economists.

291 The following article will no doubt prove an interesting contribution to this controversy.

EDWARD ATKINSON'S EVOLUTION.

[Liberty, Jan. 10, 1891.]

292 The great central principle of Anarchistic economics
—namely, the dethronement of gold and silver from their
position of command over all other wealth by the destruction
of their monopoly currency privilege—is rapidly forging to
the front. The Farmers' Alliance subtreasury scheme, un-
scientific and clumsy as it is, is a glance in this direction.
The importance of Senator Stanford's land bill, more scientific and workable, but incomplete, and vicious because gov-
ernmental, has already been emphasized in these columns.
But most notable of all is the recent evolution in the financial attitude of Edward Atkinson, the most orthodox and
cock-sure of American economists, who now swells with his
voice the growing demand for a direct representation of all
wealth in the currency.

293 In a series of articles in *Bradstreet's* and in an address before the Boston Boot and Shoe Club, this old-time
foe of all paper money not based on specie; this man who,
fifteen or twenty years ago, stood up in the town hall of
Brookline in a set debate with Col. Wm. B. Greene to com-
bat the central principle of mutual banking; this ——, who
has never lost an opportunity of insulting Anarchism and
Anarchists,—now comes forward to save the country with an
elaborate financial scheme which he offers as original with
himself, but which has really been Anarchistic thunder these
many years, was first put forward in essence by Proudhon,
the father of Anarchism, and was championed by Atkinson's
old antagonist, Col. Wm. B. Greene, to the end of his life.
Of course, all the papers are talking about it, and, on the

principle that "everything goes" that comes from the great
Atkinson, most of them give it a warm welcome, though
precious few of them understand what it means. Those
which probably do understand, like the New York *Evening
Post*, content themselves for the present with a mild protest,
reserving their heavier fire to be used in case the plan should
seem likely to gain acceptance.

294 The proposal is briefly this: that the national banks
of the country shall be divided into several districts, each dis-
trict having a certain city as a banking center; that any bank
may deposit with the clearing-house securities satisfactory to
the clearing-house committe, and receive from the clearing-
house certificates in the form of bank-notes of small denominations, to the extent of seventy-five per cent of the value of
the securities; that these notes shall bear the bank's promise
to pay on the back, and shall be redeemable on demand at
the bank in legal tender money, and, in case of failure on the
bank's part to so redeem them, they shall be redeemable at
the clearing-house; and that this new circulating medium
shall be exempt from the ten per cent tax imposed upon
State bank circulation.

295 Of course a scheme like this would not work the economic revolution which Anarchism expects from free banking. It does not destroy the monopoly of the right to bank;
it retains the control of the currency in the hands of a cabal;
it undertakes the redemption of the currency in legal tender
money, regardless of the fact that, if any large proportion of
the country's wealth should become directly represented in
the currency, there would not be sufficient legal tender money
to redeem it. It is dangerous in its feature of centralizing
responsibility instead of localizing it, and it is defective in less
important respects. I call attention to it and welcome it,
because here for the first time Proudhon's doctrine of the
republicanization of specie is soberly championed by a recognized economist. This fact alone makes it an important
sign of the times. .   .   .   .   .   .

---

296 The foregoing indicates that Mr. Atkinson's quarrel
with the Mutual Credit System is because it cannot be tacked
onto the prevailing system of money and be made to serve
the interests of the money-lenders. By his plan they could

still control and manipulate the volume of money to suit their purpose, while under the Mutual Credit System they will no longer be able to exercise that power, which, as Heywood says, "overshadows president, courts and pulpit, and is master of majorities and armies."

297   That this is the secret of Mr. Atkinson's opposition can readily be perceived.   If it is "an old familiar fallacy," why did he not point out in what the fallacy consisted? Would he not have done so if he could?   Not even when offered an opportunity to answer my reply to his rejoinder has he a word to say.   It now remains for the public to call upon these great teachers of finance to show wherein the Mutual Credit System is wrong in principle or impracticable, or confess like men that they are unable to do so.

298 Of the instruments that man has devised, money is one of the most universal of all, and its use exceeds that of any other.

299 Money and its supply bear a relation to the individual different from that of anything else. Mutual insurance, fire or life, comes, perhaps, the nearest to it. A mutual insurance company issues policies of insurance, and all to whom it issues are members, and they divide the expenses and losses upon an equitable basis, and share the advantages of protection. A mutual bank or credit association adopts the same idea of co-operation and furnishes paper money to borrowers, treating them as members, dividing the cost, and losses if there are any, and sharing the advantage of low rates of interest and plenty of money.

300 But insurance policies and paper money are totally different. The one is filed away for safe keeping and remains in its hiding place, while the other is constantly passing from hand to hand. A policy of insurance is a contract, a record of an agreement It is not in the nature of a credit, but it may become credit. It is such whenever it becomes a claim which the insurance company must meet. But until that happens it is only a promise, and one that may never mature.

301 Paper money, on the contrary, is in the nature of a credit. It is a form of credit (79-91). Not all of us are affected, except remotely, by the soundness or unsoundness of insurance. We are not all involved in the loss when an insurance company fails, but we are all affected by the character of our money. We are all involved in the risk when there is danger that our paper money will depreciate. Paper

money being credit and having no intrinsic value, is worthless when it ceases to pass in exchange for goods.   This
being the case, when we part with that which has value, to
be sure against loss, we must know that the money we take
in exchange for it will command for us the equivalent of
what we parted with.   When we purchase anything we are
generally able to judge of its value by its appearance.   Then,
again, we have some value in the material, and, except in
rare instances, the purchase is not a total loss.   We may protect ourselves by the condition that if not satisfactory, the
goods may be returned, or they may be paid for after having
been examined and found as represented.   We cannot protect
ourselves against bad money in the same way.   We could
not pay out money with the understanding that if it depreciated we would take it back and give an equivalent for it.   It
must be known to be good when taken and the transaction
must end with the acceptance of it.

302   Money is different, therefore, from all other things
we use.   We take it in exchange for everything, and for the
sole purpose of exchanging it again for everything.   We do
not do thus with anything else.   The things we take in
exchange for money are for consumption.   Money is, then,
the one universal thing which we exchange for everything
and which we exchange everything for.

303   For these reasons and for others given elsewhere (46-
51) it is the most important as well as one of the most universal instruments that we use.   There is more at stake on
this one question of money; it more deeply affects human
welfare than any other.   Policies of insurance, title deeds to
property, promissory notes of individuals, shares of stock in
corporations, like good or bad articles of merchandise, affect
only a few individuals.   Poor bread or bad water in any city
does not affect (except remotely) the people who do not live
there.   We do not get our bread and our water from one particular source.   But with money it is quite different.   It must
necessarily come from one central institution, because it must

be uniform and unquestionably reliable so that we can take it from any one who offers it, without danger of loss.

304 We are, therefore, all interested in its being reliable, and to the extent that it can be made safe, we all want plenty of it. On these two points there is no conflict of interest. It is absolutely universal, and, therefore, if there is any one enterprise that above all others should be conducted on the co-operative or mutual plan, it is the supply of money.

305 The Greenbacker, and the governmentalist and Socialists generally, advocate government control and issue of money, because that is the way co-operation develops itself in their mind (143, 144). The New Philosophy of Money teaches that co-operation can be carried on without government, and that there is no hope that government will initiate it. That the Mutual Credit System alone can put an end to interests that conflict with the general good; that they are an ever present element, a concomitant and inseparable part of government; the very object for which it exists; the sole purpose for which it was called into being and for which it is perpetuated (134, 143). That the Mutual Credit System will reduce interest to cost (95, 97, 316), and will unite in one association all women and men of business or enterprise of whatever nature, and will therefore transcend in its magnitude and importance government itself; besides, being on a business instead of a political basis, it will necessarily be conducted more economically and more honestly.*

---

* "As a comparison of the cheapness with which the government "postal monopoly," as Bro. Cunningham calls it, serves the dear people, we invite attention to its money order service, as compared with the charges and accommodations given by the express. An express money order, which costs the same as a postal money order, is good at any express office in the United States, with which the company connects, merely requiring to be properly endorsed by the payee. Thus it can be used several times in transmitting small sums, while the postal order is only good on the office it is drawn for. The consequence is that most business people patronize the express in preference to the United States postal service. There are many ways in which the regulations of the government service is such as to throw most of the business to the express companies. The United States postal service is, as most people are aware, much inferior to that of

306 It will be the carrying out the will of the people instead of that of the money power, by the only means that is practicable; for government is not only the most difficult means to employ; it is not only the hardest thing to capture in the interest of the people, but it can be recaptured by the money power. It is perpetuating a warfare with victory ever on the side of the unscrupulous; a resort to methods that are essentially reprehensible *because they rest on force and not on consent.*

307 The use of force to establish justifies its use to overthrow, and *human welfare is too precious* to depend for its realization and perpetuity on the *methods of brutes and savages.* The best system of money, when fully comprehended, will be established, not *by* government, *but in spite of it.* That tool of the money power will be used, as it ever has, not to promote the well-being of the people, but in the interest of a class.

308 The object of money being to facilitate, to expedite, and make it easy to exchange the products of labor, it follows that the best system of money is that one which will supply the money that will the most effectually accomplish this end. Now, if we were all wise as well as strictly honest, and no one would issue a promise to pay in excess of his ability to meet it, as it would be a great advantage to anyone to issue his promise to pay and obtain what he wanted by that means; and as it would also be as great an advantage to the party selling the goods, to take the promise to pay and use it as cash instead of keeping an account, which involves very much more labor and which he could not use as cash, there would be a sufficient volume of these promises to pay circulating as money, to render book credits unnecessary. Everything bought could be paid for, cash on delivery, which, to all except

the private (express) service. The express company delivers its packages to the person addressed, in the country towns as well as the cities. Why cannot the government afford to do the same thing for the same price?"—*Farm View.*

money-lenders, is a result most earnestly to be wished for.

309   It is conceded that such a system is not possible—it is not practicable—but if it would be a good system if it were practicable, what is there about it that renders it impracticable?   It certainly will not be denied that the use of money instead of book accounts is a desirable feature.   It is, however, not practicable by this method.   We lack the wisdom and the honesty to issue our promises to pay within the limits of our ability to pay.   But most people jump to the conclusion that there is no remedy for ignorance and dishonesty except to wait until people become wise and honest, and therefore it is a waste of time to look any further in this direction.

310   This is a mistake.   As well might we argue that we could not do without book accounts until memory was perfect and nothing was ever forgotten; or that the difficulty of not seeing well in a poor light could only be overcome by our vision becoming powerful enough to penetrate the darkness.

311   It is the overcoming of difficulties and avoiding of evils which exist in the very constitution of things, that diminish our burdens and adds to our comfort.   Why, then, does it not appeal to the judgment of every individual, that whoever is able and willing to assure the fulfillment of his promise to pay by pledging a sufficient amount of security, is involving no one in any risk?   The lack of wisdom and honesty to issue within limits of ability to pay, is met by a provision that limits, and the public is relieved from risk.

312   We keep accounts because memory is defective. Thus we overcome a natural difficulty; but how much better would it be to substitute money for book accounts and relieve ourselves from the labor they entail and the inconvenience of being without the goods and the money.   An argument against an individual issue of paper promises to pay, even if all were honest or if they protected holders of these promises by pledging security, is that when wanted for payment, many of them would be so far from home that they would not be

available. True enough, but this argument is not effective against the mutual system, as these individual notes do not circulate at all. Surely the intellect that has invented the differential calculus; that can foretell eclipses; that has devised bookkeeping; that can manage a clearing-house, can relieve us from such provincialism, invent a substitute to take the place of these notes in the performance of the function of money, while the notes themselves remain at home in a place of safety to be delivered up at their maturity for the substitutes that were given in exchange for them. This feature resolves another difficulty that might be argued by an opponent; that is, the great variety of notes, and, therefore, increased opportunities for counterfeiters. The substitutes can be uniform to any extent that is desirable, and, in fact, provided at a single institution for the whole country.

313 It is claimed that life insurance should be conducted on the co-operative or mutual plan; that the business of life insurance, which is to provide for those dependent loved ones when we pass to the beyond, is of too serious a character to admit of its being conducted on the ordinary methods of speculative business, and, for that reason, we especially assign to it the mutual plan, on the ground that it is safer and we run less risk. But our interest in a safe and reliable money is immeasurably greater than our interest in life insurance. Not all need to carry insurance, but everyone must use more or less money. If the argument that the mutual plan is best and safest for insurance, is sound, why is it not equally so with regard to money? If voluntary associations cannot be trusted to issue paper promises to pay in the form of money, how can they be trusted to issue paper promises to pay in the form of policies? If voluntary associations can be trusted to issue policies of insurance, they can also be entrusted with the issue of paper money. What folly to affirm that men cannot be trusted as business men, but as politicians they can! Does a bond given to government insure more faithful performance of duty than one given to a business corporation? So

far such has not been the case, of which the records of congress and the history of the government for the last thirty years afford ample proof.

314   But there is a danger in government control of money of which the people are little aware. While ample resources can be used to advantage in case of foreign invasion, which generally serves the pretext for their accumulation in the hands of government, they are ever a menace to the cause of justice. The hundreds of millions in coin piled up in the treasury are equally available against the people as they are against their enemies.* Had the Mutual Credit System prevailed, the government would have no such resources with which to attempt to enforce the unjust pretensions of the privileged class as seems likely it will. Foreign invasion is very remote, but in any event, money in the hands of people who wish to defend themselves, is just as available as it would be in the hands of the government.

315   Besides these, there are yet other considerations which we must not overlook. A permanent low and unvarying rate of interest, and a never-failing supply of money are indispensable to progress and prosperity. These being assured, enterprise can be planned much farther ahead than when the rate of interest and the supply of money is uncertain. The speculative nature of "business" will give place to an effort to excel in perfection and purity of product, the demand for such increasing as the people become prosperous. The shoddy and the adulterated will no longer satisfy, and honesty will, at last, be the best policy. The plan of the Mutual Credit System is the only one by which credit money can be substituted for commodity money and supply an unlimited volume at an unvarying rate that will not exceed cost (95, 97, 316). It entirely changes the nature of the transac-

---

* "Army officers are putting themselves to much trouble in devising means for defending Washington against a hostile fleet. If they will direct their efforts toward the discovery of some way of protecting the rest of the country against Washington they may accomplish something useful, a rare exploit for an army officer."—*Chicago Times*.

tion called borrowing money. Under the present system, the borrowing of money is regarded as borrowing capital, because of the coin basis; the borrower, although he may borrow paper money, being entitled to coin, which is wealth, while the paper is but the representative of wealth. This fact is put forward as the ground for the justification of interest; that, inasmuch as the borrower uses the capital (wealth) of another, he should pay for its use, since it enables him to gain more than he otherwise would. Even Mr. Bennett, who, as the reader has seen, is one of the most uncompromising foes of interest, says: "What is really lent is the wealth which the dollar stands for, and the dollar is used but as a measure of value" (monetary unit).* Under the Mutual Credit System, as just stated, the nature of the transaction is entirely changed; certificates of credit being furnished direct to the borrower on his security without the intervention of banker or money-lender. He is by this method relieved from the necessity of using the capital of another, availing himself of his own credit issued to him in the form of certificates (144).

316   The expense of issuing these certificates and taking care of the security, is all the borrower is called upon to pay. As evidence that this expense would be quite insignificant, let me quote Mr. A. B. Hepburn, ex-comptroller of the currency. He says in the *North American Review* for March, 1893, speaking of "the total cost to the government from all sources of the national bank system," that "an annual tax of two-fifths of one per cent upon the circulation would have defrayed all cost and redeemed all notes of all failed banks." Not only is this two-fifths of one per cent per annum sufficient to cover all expense of supervising these banks and furnish them with their paper money, but it would also have been enough to have redeemed all the notes of all the banks that failed. By adding to this the item of cost of conducting business, which, according to the commissioners of savings

---

* The attention of Mr. Bennett and of critics are especially called to paragraph 33.

banks of Massachusetts, averages in that State three-tenths of one per cent per annum, we have seven-tenths of one per cent as the total cost of furnishing paper money, taking care of the security and guaranteeing against loss. This data is the most reliable upon which to forecast the rate the Mutual Credit Associations will have to charge to cover their expenses.

317   According to the plan (see prospectus) it is proposed that the General Clearing-House Association shall supervise all the local or Mutual Credit Associations, print and furnish all the certificates of credit, guarantee holders of these certificates against their deprecjating, and insure all property pledged as security, against loss by fire or otherwise. I think that experience will prove that with the exception of the insurance of the property pledged, all the other items of expense can be covered with one-half of one per cent, for failures among the local associations, if there are any, will be insignificant compared with the failures of national banks. An average rate of insurance for the whole country, on ordinary risks, all in one association, with no extra labor for collecting than that involved in loaning the certificates of credit, as it will be included and collected with the charge made for the loan, would probably not exceed another one-half of one per cent, except for extra hazardous risks, in which case an additional charge can be made. The borrowing of money under the Mutual Credit System, then, with the very best guarantee against loss, either by depreciation of the certificates of credit or by destruction of the property by fire or otherwise would not exceed one per cent per annum.

318   This exposition of the theory upon which interest is supposed to be justifiable, conclusively proves it to be erroneous; and Mr. Bennett's statement, that "what is really lent is the wealth the dollar stands for," is not necessarily true, but only so under the present system of money.

CONCLUSION.

319 The readers who have followed closely the philosophy presented in this work, and have carefully weighed the arguments, can scarcely have failed to realize the inadequacy of the present method of exchange, with its lack of provision for a circulating medium; and many of them, if not all, will, no doubt, agree that the failure to provide this most important of all instruments is the most conspicuous fact in the study of economics; for it cannot be claimed that the mediums we have had up to the present time, have been anything but makeshifts, the parallel of which, for inconvenience and inadequacy for the function assigned it, would not have been tolerated in any mechanical enterprise since the age of invention has dawned. And that which will amaze people the most when we provide a rational system of exchange will be the enormity of the suffering mankind has endured because of the absence of so simple a device. We have national hysterics whenever manufacturers of any particular article of necessity form a trust to control the price of that article, and some of these trusts have caused nearly as much public discussion as a presidential campaign. But what are any or all of these monopolies compared with the monopoly of money? The exclusive control of one or a dozen articles is of small consequence compared with the control of the medium of exchange; yet people generally not only do not complain of the control of money, but actually think it is necessary.

320 But the failure to form correct conceptions with regard to money and how it should be supplied is not confined to the masses. "Great financiers," professors, and even money reformers by scores, fall into errors that would hardly seem possible to those making a special study of the subject.

I have endeavored to discover and point out those errors.   It
is encumbent upon some one to point out those I may have
made, and I am prepared to consider any criticisms.   One
thing is certain; the solution of the money question, popu-
larly speaking, has not yet been reached.   The ultimatum
presented by those who have acquired the greatest degree of
popularity, who have attained the most fame as writers on
banking and the money question generally, is the alternative
of performing our exchanges through the medium of coin
money, or paper money that is "redeemable in coin on demand," bartering (2, 81) one commodity for another, and
continuing the unbusinesslike credit system I have designated
as unsecured credit.   As a representative statement presenting this view, I call the reader's attention to the concluding
lines of the *Westminster Review* editorial, "Free Trade in
Banking." "Free trade principles must be applied to bank-
notes.   Every bank must be at liberty to issue them according to its means and requirements, as men in other business
are left to decide for themselves the amount of credit they
shall seek to obtain; *the sole condition required by the government being that they shall pay in coin, on demand, the
value of every note*" (323). [Italics mine.]   And also the following from the *Westminster Review's* article, "State
Tampering with Money and Banks," January, 1858:

321 "Among unmitigated rogues, mutual trust is impossible.   Among people of absolute integrity, mutual trust would
be unlimited.   These are truisms.   Given, a nation made up
entirely of liars and thieves, and all trade between its members must be carried on either by barter or by a currency of
intrinsic value; nothing in the shape of promises to pay can
pass in place of actual payments; for, by the hypothesis, such
promises being never fulfilled, will not be taken.   On the
other hand, given a nation of perfectly honest men—men as
careful of the rights of others as of their own, and nearly all
trade between its members may be carried on by memoranda
of debts and claims, eventually written off against each other
in books of bankers, seeing that, as by the hypothesis, no
man will ever issue more memoranda of debts than his goods

and his claims will liquidate, his paper will pass current for whatever it represents, coin will be needed only to furnish a measure of value and for those small transactions for which it is physically the most convenient. These we take to be self-evident truths. From these follows the obvious corrollary, that, in a nation neither wholly honest nor wholly dishonest, there may and eventually will be established a mixed currency partly of intrinsic value and partly of credit value. The ratio between the quantities of these two kinds of currency will be determined by a combination of several causes.

322   Supposing that there is no legislative meddling, which may, of course, disturb the natural balance, it is clear from what has already been said, that, fundamentally, the proportion of coin to paper will depend upon the average conscientiousness of the people. Daily experience must ever be teaching each citizen which other citizens he can put confidence in, and which not. Daily experience must also ever be teaching him how far this confidence may be carried. And thus, from personal experiment, and from current opinion which results from the experiments of others, every one must learn, more or less truly, what credit may safely be given" (329).

323   The first of these two statements imposes a condition to free trade, which is illogical. Free trade means the abolition of all restrictions or conditions on the part of government. This is conclusive, but I shall refer to it again (326, 330).

324   The next statement sustains the charge just made that the professors and popular writers know of no means of exchange except coin, paper money "redeemable in coin," or "memoranda of debts and claims eventually written off against each other in books of bankers."

325   How strange that the idea did not suggest itself to the writer of the above quotation, or some one of the many voluminous writers known to the public, that if the payment of these memoranda of debts and claims at maturity were guaranteed by a deposit of ample security, they would be fully equal if not superior, as a circulating medium, to paper money which is not thus guaranteed, but only *promised* to be redeemed in coin on demand.

326   It is perfectly evident that the *Westminster Review* knows of no means of exchange except these two: "a currency of intrinsic value"—commodity money—or "memoranda of debts and claims"—unsecured credit.* Here its resources are exhausted; its ingenuity is at an end, and, as if to prove this, it states the corrolary that naturally follows, namely, that in a community of honest and dishonest people there will be a mixed currency, partly of intrinsic value and partly of credit value, the ratio between these two depending upon the degree of honesty that prevails. Or, that if all were perfectly honest, "coin (intrinsic money) will be needed only to furnish a measure of value," etc. Now, since the Mutual Credit System will furnish certificates of credit (secured credit in the form of paper money) which are much more convenient, at less cost than "memoranda of debts and claims that have to be written off against each other in books of bankers," or any other form of unsecured credit; and infinitely more so than money of "intrinsic value," and since communities are actually made up of the honest and the dishonest, why did not the *Westminster Review* advocate the Mutual Credit System instead of paper money redeemable in coin? I have shown that the "measure of value" is only a fetish (161), and even Prof. Walker refers to it as the "so-called measure of value," so that the pretext that we need gold as money in order to have a measure of value is invalid. The fact is, it speaks to the best of its knowledge. Like all the rest of us, it is still ignorant. But what I blame it for is, that while it expresses as incomprehensible the ignorance and blunders of those who originated and still perpetuate the existing system, it fails to realize that "free trade in banking"

---

* Paper money in excess of coin actually on deposit for its redemption, is unsecured credit, and may be classed under the head of memoranda of debts and claims. Paper money for which coin to the full amount is actually held to redeem it with, may, in this case, be classed as "currency of intrinsic value," since it is not an addition thereto, but circulates exclusively in place of such currency. Hence the above statement is, strictly speaking, correct (9).

with the condition that all paper money shall be redeemable on demand, in coin, *is not free trade in banking;* that it would perpetuate the reign of the "gold bugs,"—the money power would rule just the same as it does now; that gold and silver being limited by nature, can be controlled and cornered, and that those who *must have it* would still be at the mercy of those who *have it;* that while it realizes and so skilfully points out the evils we endure and the cause that produced them, it fails to provide a remedy; and when a remedy is offered it fails to accept it or point out wherein it is defective. In 1889, before I published "Citizens' Money," seeing that it advocated less restriction in the supply of money and attributed depression in trade to the lack of freedom in exchange, I mailed to the editor of that journal a type-written copy. About a year after, it was returned to me with a polite note stating that he could not use it. What can the *Westminster Review* say now about those whom it accuses of what itself is guilty—its infatuation about the need of a coin basis, while its own statements prove the absurdity of its position? Speaking of the demonetization of silver in England, it says: "The infatuation of this step it is impossible to appreciate or account for. Continually the scarcity of money had produced the same disastrous results. There was a panic from this cause in 1793 and it could only be relieved by the issue of £5,000,000 in Exchequer Bills; and in 1811 a similar crisis occurred which was relieved by the same means." A money panic is relieved and comes to an end by the British treasury issuing bills to private parties on liens on their fixed property. Does it not follow that if merchants, manufacturers and other business men form an association whose sole object shall be to furnish a medium of exchange by the issue of bills, not only on fixed property (except vacant land) but also on warehouse receipts, and which bills all the members of the association bind themselves to take in payment of debt at their face value, and in exchange for commodities without discrimination in prices, that such a system would put an end to a money panic equally as well, and that if all money was thereafter furnished by this means, no subsequent panic could possibly occur?

327 There is no foundation whatever for the notion that paper money issued by government is more reliable than by the plan I propose. The Populists will probably make use of this item about the relief afforded by the Exchequer issuing paper money to private parties (if they have not already done so), but to do it for temporary relief, and to make a permanent thing of it, are quite different. In the case of temporary issue, the speculators have not time to get in their work; besides the amount furnished was a bagatelle compared with the whole amount that would be issued under the subtreasury proposition. Then, again, the Exchequer Bills were issued at headquarters only, whereas the subtreasury scheme contemplates the issue of government paper money in every city, thus multiplying the opportunities for corruption as the number of cities in the United States are to one. Will it be pretended that a comparatively few individuals, and these politicians, calling themselves *the government*, assuming control of the issue of money, themselves to determine on what, and to attempt to force it into circulation by making it legal tender, would be a more satisfactory method and afford greater responsibility than an organization established upon a commercial basis, with its local associations in every city and a general clearing-house for all of them; its money not legal tender, but circulating on its merits, the whole membership having bound themselves to accept it?

328 What has got into people in the United States within the last few years, that in proportion as the government becomes corrupt, disregards their rights and proves that its control of money is incompatible with progress or prosperity —they insist upon its offices, its intermeddling? But more of this hereafter.

329 Referring again to the *Westminster Review:* The incongruity of the disjointed, unsecured credit system of today

could not be better illustrated than it has been by this journal. "Daily experience must ever be teaching each citizen which other citizens he can put confidence in, and which not. Daily experience must also ever be teaching him how far this confidence may be carried. And thus, from personal experiment and from current opinion which results from the experiments of others, every one must learn, more or less truly, what credit may safely be given." Alas for human happiness! Where we looked for wisdom, we found foolishness, where we expected honey, we were given wormwood and gall. Why must we be forever learning, forever experimenting to reach the unattainable? The teaching we get from daily experience is, that confidence cannot with safety be given under the corrupting system the money power has fastened upon us. Every one has learned more or less sorrowfully that the only credit that can with safety be given is *secured credit* (83); and why should we have any other? The peurility of this reasoning is simply amazing. We are offered the consolation that during a lifetime we may find some by whom our confidence was not betrayed or who were successful and could afford to be honest; but how about the dishonest, the wrecks, the victims of monopoly, of sharpers, and those who are thrown out of employment, from whom this proposition offers no deliverance?

330 All these evils are the effects of the prevailing unsecured credit system, which, in turn, is the result of the monopoly of money. Instead of removing the monopoly by dissociating government from supplying or regulating money and substituting for the present system a rational system of secured credit, it is proposed to extend unsecured credit by the unrestricted issue of paper money purporting to be redeemable in coin on demand; the government to see that this condition is complied with. On the first page of its article, "Free Trade in Banking, it defines free trade: "The principle is right—perfect freedom of exchange between nations and individuals." And in the face of this definition it pro-

poses the issue of paper money, government to see that those who issue it redeem it in coin whenever it is demanded. This restriction limits freedom, and is therefore not "perfect freedom." But the *Review* has got into a dilemma on another point also, from which it will be equally hard to extricate itself. It is evident that we could not have any more paper than there is coin under the method proposed, without the issuers taking the chances of being called upon to furnish something they do not possess. The following is its own language: "The supply of gold and silver has long been inadequate to the requirements of commerce. Even with all the forms of paper currency, still the gold produced has been insufficient for the growing wants of the world." We are told that there is not enough gold and silver to supply a sufficient volume of money, and that the way to have the deficiency supplied is to leave each banker to determine for himself to what extent he is willing to take the chances of being caught with less coin than he has agreed to pay on demand. That they must resort to this overissue to avoid a scarcity of money, needs no proof. That they would all take chances no one will for a moment doubt. For an individual or several of them to be able to loan their unsecured credit to responsible parties on good security, and get good pay for doing so, is too much of a temptation to be resisted. If this paper is taken by everybody and no one demands coin, or not enough to require interference on the part of government, business will go on with a rush for a time, but the inevitable result would be an enormous inflation of paper money. The indifference on the part of the people to demand coin would encourage an ever-increasing overissue, as the drawing of interest on one's promise to pay is so alluring; so that a final crash would be certain and unavoidable. There would be a run on most of the banks and the great majority of them would go under. If, on the other hand, the people were constantly to demand coin, very little increase in the volume of money would take place and we should continue to suffer from a dearth of money.

331 Reduced to its last analysis, then, the *Westminster Review's* proposition affords us the alternatives: paralysis of business from lack of money, continued poverty, crime and revolution; or inflation, wildcat banking, wild speculation, a general crash, blasted hopes, pandemonium, poverty, crime, and, finally, also revolution. But if bankers may issue paper money redeemable in coin, why may not merchants, manufacturers and others, issue paper money redeemable in other products? The bills issued by bankers are the banker's credit, and *they are unsecured credit*. If bankers may use their credit wherever they can, why may not everyone else do the same? Why do not people see that if this right were recognized and government ceased entirely from meddling in the matter, the very importance of the question would call forth the best talent to devise a system that would be satisfactory. If the Mutual Credit System can be improved upon, no one could prevent it and all would be benefited by the improvement. Free trade in banking means that every one has the right to issue his own money and pass it out into circulation as best he can. If this right (and it is but one's right to his credit) were suddenly demanded by the majority, and all restrictions were wiped off the statute books, and people commenced offering their paper money, the boards of trade in every city would at once call meetings to devise means for providing a reliable and uniform medium of exchange. All business men and women would be aroused to a profound and exhaustive discussion of the money question. All sides would then get a fair hearing; the best system would naturally come to the surface, and the fittest would survive. If we did not get a perfect system at first improvements would be added, because, as stated elsewhere (301-304) it is the one thing in which all producers and exchangers of products are mutually interested; there is no conflict of interest whatever; the only interest antagonized would be the money-lenders'. The establishment of the best system is as

certain, therefore, as the continuance of the human race.*

332   But there is another point we must not overlook in the issue of bills by bankers as proposed by the *Westminster Review*. These bankers would either hold coin to the amount of bills issued or they would not. If they did, how would we avoid scarcity of money? But, as, of course, they would not, it follows that the bills they issue are *their unsecured credit*. How inconceivably stupid! All those who have good security, instead of forming into a solid financial institution to issue bills against the security they actually possess, by a method that would be safe and satisfactory to everybody, and which could not possibly be manipulated or entail loss upon any one, are coerced into helping the banker draw interest on what he does not possess. In other words, instead of each using his own individual *secured credit* at one per cent or less, he has to pay from 6 to 100 per cent for the *unsecured credit* of some one else. Thus the banker lives on the interest on what he owes, and the public takes the chances of his paying his debts. We may laugh at the absurdity, but it is precisely what we have been doing since the invention of paper money. The money-lenders have deluded the people into believing in the "standard of value" fake, and have thus controlled the enormous advantage of paper money in their own interest; whereas, if paper money had been used in the interest of the borrower since the date of its invention, we should not now be mourning poverty, corruption, vice and crime. The policeman's club would be a museum curiosity, and the gatling gun never would have been invented. There never would have been any call for it. There are other criticisms that might be fairly made of the *Westminster Review's* article; but the one purpose for which it was repro-

---

* At the recent annual meeting of the American Association for the Advancement of Science, vice-president Farquhar, in his address in the section of economic science and statistics, upon a State monetary unit, favored the abandonment of attempts to establish a legal tender by legislation, and the leaving of the question to settle itself. —*Popular Science Monthly, October, 1893.*

duced, namely, to show in an authentic manner a history of money panics, and the effects of money monopoly—the acts of government—in England, has been accomplished. My criticisms are made with a view of pointing out the errors of the old and proving the correctness of the new philosophy of money.

333 As a specimen of the same kind of reasoning and of the absence of a real appreciation of what is needed, I will now present a statement from another source—an extract from a recent pamphlet, entitled "Bimetallism," by Prof. Francis A. Walker, author of "Money," "Political Economy," and several other works; superintendent of the United States Census of 1880, and president of the Massachusetts Institute of Technology. "My subject is Bimetallism. It is not to be disguised that there is, on the part of many public-spirited citizens here at the east, a certain indisposition to consider this subject at the present time, a shrinking from the questions it involves. The reasons for this are not far to seek. In the first place, many, in opposing the free coinage of silver and working for the repeal of the purchase clauses of the Sherman Act, have thrown themselves naturally, though by no means logically, into an attitude of antagonism towards silver, which is not in conformity with the traditions of the American people, and which they would not have taken but for the severe struggle of the last three years, and especially of the past summer. In the second place, people are tired and worn out with the still recent contest over free coinage and the purchase of silver bullion, ·and want a rest from the subject. This mental attitude, again, is natural enough, but it is, nevertheless wrong. *No question is ever settled until it is settled right.* The repeal of the purchase clauses of the Sherman Act settled nothing. It but opened the way for a proper treatment of the financial problem. *That problem must be grappled with until it is solved.* There is neither statesmanship nor

good citizenship in seeking to evade or procrastinate the issue it presents.

334 "Another cause which helps to produce a certain indisposition to consider the silver question is found in the apprehension of many persons well inclined towards bimetallism, that to raise this issue will excite our fellow-citizens at the south and west and increase their urgency for free coinage. This view is held in good faith, but I must regard it as wholly mistaken. Our southern and western friends have got hold of a half truth, or rather a half truth has got hold of them, and has produced among them something very like a fanaticism dangerous to the republic. The half of the truth regarding money which actuates the south and west is that a diminishing money supply constitutes a great evil. The way in which the gold monometallists seek to meet this is by opposing to it a half truth of their own, namely, that an inflated, depreciated and rapidly fluctuating money is a fruitful source of social and industrial mischief. But a half truth which excites to fanaticism has never yet been successfully opposed by another half truth appealing to conservatism. The only way to meet the dangerous demands from the west and south, *is by telling and urging the whole truth*, which in this matter is found in bimetallism—bimetallism on a broad, international basis, which would both secure the desired stability of the so-called standard of value and prevent the incontestable evils of a diminishing money supply." [The italics are mine.]

335 Mr. Walker's remedy for the scarcity of money is international bimetallism. That is to say, he believes in co-operating with other nations with a view of bringing silver coin into more general use, so as to have more money without depreciation. Of course the inevitable corollary follows, even if it were for a moment conceded to be a remedy, that if other nations will not co-operate, we have no alternative but to go on with the limited volume of money that periodically paralyzes production and exchange.

To what a pass have we come! It is not Nature that has placed obstacles in the way of continued production and exchange, but man's cupidity on the one hand and his ignorance on the other. Nature is always ready to serve us if we only adopt her methods. But in matters of exchange we proceed in open violation of her teachings, as we learn from the records of the past and from observation. We make an arbitrary, artificial regulation that is impossible to be complied with. The use of gold and silver as media of exchange is not a condition imposed by Nature. It is a superstition that dominates men, that such media is necessary. They declare that these metals must be the basis of exchange, and persist in perpetuating the absurdity, although every money panic is traced to this as the cause. There is not enough; and if a sufficient amount were found to give us plenty of money at present weight and value of coin, it would not afford us relief, because Nature's methods—supply and demand—cannot be set aside, and the purchasing power of the coin would diminish precisely in proportion to the increase in the supply. This cannot be denied either by the monometallists or the bimetallists, for it is one of their cardinal doctrines that "increase in the volume of money reduces its purchasing power." They nevertheless persist, and until we emancipate ourselves from their control of money we must endure the penalty. In the whole domain of human activities, inventive genius is prompt with needed innovations, but conservatism stands guard on the highways of exchange, lest iconoclastic reform should demolish its golden calf.

Bonum magis carendo quam fruendo, cernitur.

336 Man never *is*, but always *to be* blessed. If the rocks would only cease to yield the "precious" metals, this might be changed. We should then have neither monometallists nor bimetallists, and rational views on the subjects of money and value might be confidently looked for, even among the professors and "great financiers." As the "stand-

ard of value" we are *said* to have could not then exist, they
might "catch on" to the fact that the monetary unit, and not
a measure or standard, is the means by which we comprehend and express relative value; that when we are told the
value of this object is five dollars, and of that, three dollars,
and of another, two dollars, we have no difficulty in forming
a clear conception of what it is intended to convey, of the
relative value of these different articles. And, of course, the
same is true of the fractions of the monetary unit—cents—as
of the unit itself. Value being only a relation, if all parties
express value by means of the same term as the monetary
unit, there cannot possibly be any misunderstanding. This
term—the monetary unit—is but an abstraction. Value being established by supply and demand, we can, by the use of
this unit, from its smallest fraction to any multiple of the
unit itself, express value to any amount. And I most emphatically declare, without fear of successful refutation, that
it never has been anything else but an abstraction since the
invention of paper money, just the same as it undoubtedly is
in bookkeeping "money of account," so-called. That monometallism and bimetallism, instead of helping to convey a
definite idea of value by establishing a "measure" or "standard" of value, are but a disturbing element in value in exchange.* That previous to the invention of paper money,
all exchanges were in the nature of barter. The people
exchanged commodities for commodity money, which is an
exchange of values, and is therefore barter (81, 88). We
use the term, dollar, because it is more convenient than it
would be to express value in the smallest fraction; in which
case we should need no term, but simply say one, or any
multiple of one. Thus one hundred would be what we now
mean when we say one dollar; 500, five dollars; 5,000, fifty
dollars; 5,678, fifty-six dollars and seventy-eight cents and so
on. The prevailing method of conveying from one mind to

---

* See foot-note, page 94.

another the value of objects being satisfactory, we effect exchanges of values by one of two methods, barter or credit. Barter is the exchange of one object of value for another object of value. To exchange for coin, therefore, is a species of barter. To exchange for paper money is a credit transaction, because paper money is a form of credit. It is distinguished from ordinary credit which is not a settlement on the spot, by designating it secured credit (82, 84). If we express the value of all objects and divide up secured credit and issue it in the form of paper money, using the same denominator or monetary unit in both cases, any given amount of either must be equivalent to the same amount of the other; and if this secured credit is redeemed at its face value in any commodity at its market value, it can be transferred from one to another with perfect safety. We only need, then, to provide for its redemption to make its use perfectly safe. We have no need, therefore, of a coin made of a definite quantity of some special metal to inform us how much is a dollar's worth, for we can ascertain that fact by consulting a price list; the market value of a commodity will always give us the exact amount that can be had for a dollar. The amount of gold a paper dollar (that is, secured credit) will buy, is a dollar's worth of gold, and so with all other articles or commodities. The essential item, with the exception of precautions against counterfeiting, is the provision, when the secured credit is granted, that its redemption at its face value and at the time agreed upon, be imperative and unavoidable. Under such a system there can be no disturbing element in value, such as gold is and always has been.

337 The advantage that the Mutual Credit System possesses in the matter of redemption of secured credit is that parties can redeem the amount of secured credit that has become due, by exchanging anything they can for it, instead of being compelled to furnish a definite quantity of some special commodity, as is the case when paper money is issued on gold and the gold is demanded. What constitutes a dollar's

11

worth, then, in any commodity, is the amount of that commodity that is offered in exchange for a dollar of secured
credit.   What constitutes a "dollar" of secured credit is the
certificate of credit of that denomination that is issued by
the Mutual Credit Association, and which, therefore, the
party who obtained it from that association has pledged
himself to redeem with one dollar's worth of market value,
and has guaranteed that he will fulfil that pledge by depositing a sufficient amount of security.   So with all certificates
of credit, of whatever denomination.

338   But to return again to the subject of Prof. Walker's
pamphlet, we must confess that he says some good things.
For instance: "No question is ever settled until it is settled
right." . . "That [financial] problem must be grappled
with until it is solved. There is neither statesmanship nor
good citizenship in seeking to evade or procrastinate the issue
it presents."   These statements express the right sentiment,
and it is to be hoped that he will neither evade nor procrastinate the issue herein brought to his notice.   Why the fact
that a diminishing money supply constitutes a great evil, and
that an inflated, depreciated and rapidly fluctuating money is
a fruitful source of social and industrial mischief, should be
called "half truths," is not clear.   They are each of them
whole truths of the most vital importance.   But does Prof.
Walker comprehend the real issue this financial problem presents?   It would seem that "public-spirited citizens at the
east," as elsewhere, who "shrink from the question it involves," have a keener insight into the "issue it involves" than
has Prof. Walker; and that he attributes their indisposition to
a wrong cause.   The real issue, Prof. Walker, is the wresting
from government its usurped power of the control and regulation of the supply of money.   The speculating capitalist
sees this sooner than the professors do.   To them (the capitalists) this is the "fanaticism that is dangerous to the republic,"—the republic that has built them up and crushed the
toiler.   But a republic is only an institution.   Why does

Prof. Walker manifest so much concern about an institution? Are institutions more sacred,—are they still, at this late day paramount to the liberty and prosperity of the people? Take away the people's credit, give it into the hands of a few to be farmed out at their discretion, and your republic, or whatever you call your political organization, is doomed. And it is right that it should be. Man and his well-being is the subject to consider,—not institutions. They are ever changing and necessarily must change as man progresses. He must change his institutions to suit his wants, or cease to progress in order to remain in conformity with his institutions. Which shall it be?

339 Discussing the effect of law upon value, Prof. Walker says: "As regards bimetallism, then, the question simply is: Can government set in motion any economic force which will affect the relative values of gold and silver? I answer, yes, incontestably; and that force is one of enormous scope and reach. By declaring the two metals indifferently legal tender in the payment of debts, at a certain ratio, it can at once and powerfully influence the demand for one and the other of the two metals. This was exactly what France did by the law of 1803, which established the bimetallic system. By that law France declared that an ounce of gold, in coined money, should have precisely the same power to pay debts as that possessed by fifteen and one-half ounces of silver, in coined money. The operation of this principle was simple, instantaneous, automatic and of overwhelming force." Evidently Prof. Walker is not an evolutionist, or he would not trammel progress with government supervision and dictation. If there never had been government control of money, there would never have been a money panic. The inventive ingenuity of man would never have tolerated a scarcity of money if superstition that government must control money had not dominated him. Scarcity of money is the effect of law. Men have more respect for law than for their rights. Otherwise they would not tolerate laws

that interfere with their rights. The class that own all the gold and silver coin, the money-lenders—and who are always the ruling class—procure the enactment of laws compelling the use of coin as money, the legal tender clause being their trump card. They make us use their coin, and the tribute they levy on us for its use is more than the net increase of wealth (121). Of course they do not take more than the net increase. It would be difficult for them to get more than there is, but they demand all that, and their watch-dog, that the people have elected to govern, see that they get it. Gold monometallism means that those who own the gold coin want a monopoly of this lucrative business. Bimetallism means that those interested in silver want a share of the spoils. The people will have to repudiate both or abandon all hope of liberty. Prof. Walker is wrong. Government can set in motion a force, but it is not an economic force; it is the effect of arbitrary interference with economic force. All interference with natural and free exchange will affect relative values, but by what right government may thus interfere with demand and supply he does not say. That governments can call into play, in monetary affairs, a force of "enormous scope and reach," let the following extract from the *Westminster Review* testify.

340   "Lord Ashburton, one of its [the Bank of England] prime champions, said: 'Our monetary laws put it in the power of a few shrewd capitalists so to contract the supply of gold as to embarrass the bank and nearly ruin the nation.' [They have done the same in this country and have completely ruined the "nation."—Author.] Lord Overstone, another advocate of the system, said: 'Against the actual exhaustion of its treasures, through foreign exchange, the bank has the power of protecting itself. But to do this, she must produce a pressure upon the money market, ruinous for its suddenness and severity. She must save herself by the ruin of all around her'." Without extending our inquiry further, it has been clearly demonstrated that the two nations

which boast of being the foremost in civilization,— the
United States and Great Britain—both, by the monopoliza-
tion of the medium of exchange have instituted and perpetuated poverty, and, consequently, all its concomitant evils,—
misery, immorality and crime. The amount of mental and
physical torture thus inflicted by government, we shall never
know. Instead, therefore, of government meriting our ad-
miration and respect, as the votaries of authority and force
claim it should, after a thorough examination of the subject
it calls forth a most profound, solemn and spontaneous exe-
cration.

341 Does the reader want more evidence? He shall have
it, and from this same Francis Amasa Walker. "Look at
the financial and industrial history of the past few years!
Everywhere the stockholder is giving way to the bondholder;
everywhere we hear of receiverships; everywhere the mort-
gagee is coming into possession; everywhere the weight of
the dead hand is felt continually increasing." That Gen.
Francis Amasa Walker is innocent of any knowledge of the
crime and usurpation of government in controlling and limiting the supply of money is proved by another statement
he makes: "There will be panics, crises and hard times
under any system." Now, bear in mind that this statement
comes from a man on whom the degree of A. M. was conferred by Amherst College, in 1863, and by Yale College in
1873. Later, these same institutions honored him with the
Ph. D. and L. L. D.; Harvard in 1883, Columbia in 1887,
and St. Andrew's, Scotland, in 1888. He was United States
Commissioner to the International Monetary Conference in
Paris, in 1878, and was elected the same year to the National
Academy of Sciences. Is president of the American Statistical Society and of the American Economic Association, and
also an honorary fellow of the Royal Statistical Society of
London. I mean no disrespect to this "honorary fellow";
on the contrary, I wish to show that he is no worse than
other college-bred men whose early training is a process of

literary cramming instead of developing individuality and
independence of thought, by which means evolution of right
and the triumph of justice would come in their natural order.
But, instead, error holds the fort against fact, dogma wields
a club, reason is prostrate and brutal conflict seems inevitable.
France did not solve the economic question by the establishment of the bimetallic system in 1803, and which lasted
about seventy years; it having been abandoned in 1874.
Neither does Mr. Walker expect it would if reestablished,
for he says: "There will be panics and hard times under
any system." What, then, have we to hope for from the
bimetallic system?   Mr. Bennett has demonstrated that interest is impossible.   I have shown that it can be abolished.
Mr. Walker ignores the issue.   In 1888 I mailed him a type-
written copy of my essay, "Citizens' Money."   Later, I
received a note from him, stating that our views on the issue
of paper money were so far apart that it was useless to discuss it.   Mr. Walker mourns over the financial and industrial history of the past few years, and offers only a palliative
that is impracticable and announces a remedy impossible.
Yet the system herein proposed, the very one he would not
condescend to discuss, is a practicable and effectual remedy
for all currency evils, as time will prove.

342   Another professor whom I am called upon to criti-
cize is William W. Folwell, of the University of Minnesota,
who also refused to discuss the merits of the Mutual Credit
System.   This gentleman has quite a reputation in the north-
west as a political economist; was at one time president of
the University.   I called on him soon after I commenced
my propaganda work in this vicinity, had a pleasant talk
with him and presented him with copies of my two pamphlets, with the understanding that he would give me a written
expression of his opinion in regard to the new money system
they proposed.   About six months passed, during which
time I did not hear from him.   I then called on him, and
also once since then, but I could get nothing definite or satis-

factory from him; his excuse being that he had been too busy with his duties, but he promised each time to give the matter his attention as soon as circumstances would permit. About the 1st of March, 1894, I wrote him a note inviting him to address the Financial Club on the subject of the Mutual Credit System. The following is his reply:

MINNEAPOLIS, MINN., March 8, 1894.

MY DEAR SIR:

Your favor has remained unanswered because I have been busied with my college examinations and was out of town over Sunday.

I am obliged to decline your polite invitation to address the Financial Club on the subject named, because I cannot now take time from my duties to make the necessary investigation.

I must confess that I am strongly prejudiced in favor of hard money, chiefly because it accomplishes instant liquidation and saves account keeping. For this reason, alone, I am of opinion that for an indefinite time, civilized men will use it as an instrument of exchange.

Very truly yours,

WILLIAM W. FOLWELL.

343 By "hard money," of course the professor means coin. He confesses he is "strongly prejudiced in favor of hard money, chiefly because it accomplishes instant liquidation and saves account keeping." Now, the facts are, that while it is true that hard money accomplishes instant liquidation in the individual cases in which it is used, it is also true that all business transactions cannot be thus liquidated with hard money, because there is not enough of it for that purpose, and, in the very nature of things, there never can be (335); and it is for this reason that the Mutual Credit System was devised and is offered as a substitute, because it will facilitate the accomplishment of instant liquidation in *all business transactions*. It is not true, therefore, that, as a system, hard money accomplishes instant liquidation and saves account keeping; for it is the hard money system that com-

pels a resort to account keeping and other forms of unsecured credit, and from which there is no relief except by the
adoption of the Mutual Credit System.

344   In the light of these facts, which have been amply
sustained in this volume, what is the position of Prof. Folwell?   His position is that of one who is ignorant and prejudiced on the subject; the subject being the very one for
which he holds a professorship and about which he presumes
to instruct the youths who attend the University.   He is
called upon and it is pointed out to him that he is teaching
that which is not true, and is furnished with printed matter
that claims to prove this position.   He is respectfully invited
to express his opinion and is afforded an opportunity to lec-
ture on the subject but declines to do so.   He is next included
in a general challenge to meet the writer in a public debate;
but there is no response.   Evidently, the question whether
he is teaching correct ideas or not, is of little consequence to
him.   If it is error, it is at least respectable and venerable,
and he has plenty of company, since the professors in all the
colleges are teaching the same error.

345   Let me now call the reader's attention to a few popular fallacies we have not heretofore considered.   One of
these fallacies is the popular notion that as gold and also silver coin is shipped abroad to settle balances due other nations, that we actually settle such balances with money just
as banks settle balances through the clearing-houses with
money.   This notion is erroneous.   The coin shipped is
accepted, not as money, but as commodity.*   It is so much
gold or so much silver.   The stamp which government impresses upon the coin is useful in that it is acceptable proof
of the degree of fineness or purity of the metal it is composed

---

* Wm. P. St. John, president of the Mercantile Nat. Bank of New
York, in his testimony before the Committe on Currency and Banking, Said: "Money is all domestic.   Our $10 gold piece is accounted
258 grains of nine-tenths fine gold when beyond the jurisdiction of
the United States." [When of full weight, Mr. St. John should have
added.]

of, but it does not affect its value; that is determined by what gold or silver is worth on the market as bullion. We do not, therefore, pay foreign balances with money at its face value. We may ship money, but we must send enough to make up the difference between the face value and the bullion value of the coin, as the latter is what counts.† If the clearing-house in New York, through which most foreign balances are paid, has coin of the particular nation to which a balance is due, it can ship that coin, and that, of course, is accepted at its face value because it is the money of that nation. The same is true when a foreign clearing-house has a balance to pay the clearing-house in New York and has coin of this nation. It is, of course, accepted at its face value. Coin, therefore, when it leaves the country that coined it, goes as commodity, but when it returns, it returns as money.

346 It will be seen, then, that coin is not essential to pay foreign balances, and that the establishment of the Mutual Credit System will not in the least interfere with such settlements. Foreign debt being always paid in commodities, *what* commodity depends on which it is the most profitable to ship. When the Mutual Credit System has effectually put an end to manipulations of the money market by speculators, these balances will adjust themselves, mostly, perhaps entirely, by exchange of products for consumption, instead of constantly carting gold or silver back and forth between nations, merely for the purpose of settling balances due. Bullion, and also coin, is sometimes shipped out one week and returned the next. Interest on a few millions, even for a few days, is considerable of an item, and it is to avoid payment of interest that this bullion is hurried forward to meet obligations when they become due; but when the Mutual

---

† With this exception, however, that a balance due a nation creates a demand for its coin, because it can be used as money to pay that balance, provided it is full weight, and therefore enhances its value above that of bullion.

Credit System shall have annihilated that hydra-headed monster begotten of stupidity and law, there will be greater latitude in the settlement of balances, admitting of their liquidation by the shipment of other commodities, the freight and insurance on which will not be a useless expense.

347   Another popular fallacy is the prevailing notion that the existence of the wildcat banks of ante bellum times was due to lack of government control of banking; and the fact that they disappeared after the federal government assumed control is pointed to as proof that the notion is correct. Not long ago a southern daily paper, discussing the subject, made the following statement:

348   "The wildcat bank is an institution which springs up in the absence of good currency, and under such conditions, if the wildcat did not come, there would be an equivalent in unsecured book credits. Liberty to organize for the issue of sound currency is the extinguisher to be placed upon all schemes for issuing wildcat paper."

349   This is the correct idea. If the people had thoroughly understood the money question, they would have organized to supply themselves with a medium of exchange that was reliable, and refused to take that which was doubtful, for no one was compelled to take the "money" of the wildcat banks. Such a course would have effectually exterminated them. But money was scarce then as it is now, and the ignorance of the people afforded an opportunity for unprincipled speculators to float their worthless bills. If there had been plenty of money as easily obtainable as it will be under the Mutual Credit System, it would have been impossible for "wildcat" or "red-dog" "money" to have got into circulation.

350   But other speculators, just as unprincipled, devised a scheme to get rid of the wildcat by forming a money trust, with government to enforce its demands. Thus the centralization of the money power under the protection of the general government was consummated. Then the promoters of

this scheme went about boasting that they had rid the country of wildcats, and established the "best money system the world has ever seen." It was not to increase the volume of money that they did this, but to cut off the competition that such banks made the "regular" bankers. It would be interesting to know whether the people have not lost more by the failures of national banks than they ever did by the wildcats. For the four years preceding 1890, the loss to depositors by failures of national banks exceeded a million dollars a year. Recent inquiry at the comptroller's department failed to ascertain what the loss has been since then.*

351 Necessity, not government, is the mother of invention. Ingenuity is the originator of remedies or means of overcoming difficulties. The quickest and surest way, then, to have evils removed, is to encourage ingenuity to invent means of overcoming them. This is the course that should be pursued instead of allowing government to interfere. It involves no compulsory contributions for experiment. Those who wish to experiment, do so at their own expense. Government being in reality but the watch-dog and tool of the class that has succeeded in getting control, instead of invent-

---

* Mr. Geo. A. Butler, president of the National Tradesmen's Bank of New Haven, Connecticut, testified before the Congressional Committee on Banking and Currency, December 12, 1894, as follows:

As to the guarantee fund, I made some figures embracing twenty-nine years of the national banking system. Take all the national banks that have failed within that twenty-nine years and if you had not only made the notes payable out of this guarantee fund, but the deposits also, that fund would have paid every dollar lost by depositors as well as every dollar of notes, and there would have been more than two and a half times the amount left in the treasury. In other words, in the twenty-nine years the banks have paid in to the government seventy-nine millions as a tax on their circulation, and if that had been applied to paying the depositors in failed banks as well as the notes of failed banks, it would have paid every dollar of it and still left fifty-two millions in the treasury."

Since this tax was collected to cover expenses of supervision and thus protect (?) *the people* against wildcat banking, and since it did not make good the losses to depositors of failed national banks, but held onto the plunder,—the excess over cost of "supervision"—the government must be regarded as *particeps criminis* with those who robbed the depositors.

ing a remedy for an evil, it devises a scheme in the interest of
that class, labels it a "remedy" and foists it upon the people,
who, supposing government to be the paternalistic institution
they have been led to believe, neglect to analyze its true character. After time has proved the "remedy" does not give
the results anticipated, they conclude it is because the wrong
men are in office and that others must be put in their place;
but the change, instead of affording relief only intensifies the
evils. A new combination of speculators and politicians is
formed. "Now we have the pop-sure thing!" It looks
plausible on its face, because of the peculiarly illogical way
people have of reasoning,—the result of a false education
which suppresses manhood and independence and cultivates
obedience and respect for authority, instead of for that which
is right. In the meantime, the inventor, the genius who
could afford relief by organizing associations to put in operation practical remedies, is handicapped by the restrictions the
class in control have instituted in the name of "law and order," "good government" and the like, when, in reality, it is
done to prevent the people from freeing themselves from the
slavery they are in.

352   If the people possessed sufficient manhood and independence, the functions of government would constantly be
reduced, and the evils we are contending with would be
overcome in the same proportion.   Freedom to devise ways
and means to improve our condition is what we need, and it
can only come in proportion as politicians cease to rule.

353   Among the fallacies, or at least mistaken notions of
reform, is that of regarding the land question as paramount
to the money question. This view is not confined to the
Single Taxers. It is held also by others who are not, but
who would abolish all titles to land except for actual use.
Prominent among the latter is Mr. J. K. Ingalls, who has
written very ably on free land. Of so little importance does
this writer regard the money question, that in his pamphlet,

"Work and Wealth," treating of industrial emancipation, the following is all he has to say about it:

354 "I may, in this connection, refer to the instrumentality of money or currency, servicable in moving crops and the work of distributing generally. Its importance, however, is mainly due to the want of mutualism in our distributive system and of equity in our methods of exchange.

355 "A charge for the time use of this instrument, in defiance of all the moralists from Moses and Cato to Ruskin and Palmer, has been enforced by our laws, because labor was at the mercy of the few who hold the soil, and because operations could be made to pay dividends out of the wealth purchased by the labor of the poor and simple."

356 The Mutual Credit System is the very essence of mutualism in distribution, and its realization is the only possible way of introducing equity into our methods of exchange. It is not the importance of money, therefore, that is "mainly due to the want of mutualism in our distributive system," but the unnatural, artificial power that money now possesses (359), for the certificates of credit or money of the Mutual Credit Associations, will be the most important factor in our distributive system. If Mr. Ingalls knows of a plan by which mutualism and equity can be introduced into our methods of exchange, and in which money will become an unimportant factor, he should give it to the public. It is true, as he says, interest "has been enforced by our laws"; but when he says, "because labor was at the mercy of those who hold the soil," he has ventured into deep water without knowing how to swim. Did the fact that labor was at the mercy of those who hold the soil enable the money-lenders to enforce interest by law? Suppose the land question settled, and anyone can occupy or utilize vacant land without having to buy or pay rent, would they not enforce interest by law just the same as they do now if the money system remains unchanged? Will free land abolish interest on capital invested otherwise than in land? Will it put an end to interest on national, county, state and municipal debts? Will the money-lender

loan his money at a less rate of interest because monopoly of
land has come to an end?   Mr. Ingalls and those of his
school seem to think that when the abolition of land monopoly is attained, very little money will be needed; it will become a drug in the market and thus interest will disappear.
This reasoning is utterly absurd.   What will induce people
to abandon the use of money?   Nothing but a system of
exchange that will dispense with the use of money.   But
such a system would have to be superior in every way and
more economical than any that has been or could be devised
that used money;   and until land reformers and Single Taxers, who belittle the importance of money, can show us such
a system, it would be an advantage to the cause they are interested in if they would reconsider their philosophy on the
subject.   They should give good reasons for their position or
abandon it.

357   The money question and the land question are separate and distinct questions.   Either can be settled without the
other, although the settlement of one would greatly facilitate
the settlement of the other, because the struggle to get rid of
the one would naturally open the eyes and the understanding
of the people to the evils of, and the proper remedy for, the
other.   If the solution and settlement of either will contribute to the solution and settlement of the other, the question
to consider first, is, which of the two is the easiest of accomplishment?   To this, most, if not all philosophical Anarchists
will answer,—"the money question," and these are their reasons: The settlement of the land question requires legislation, or revolution dispossessing the landlords by force.   The
former is out of the question at present.   Civil war is immi-
nent, and may happen in the near future; but it is very
undesirable and should be avoided if possible.   On the other
hand, the settlement of the money question, as "The New
Philosophy of Money" has demonstrated, is a question of
organizing a few associations upon an equitable and practicable basis.   The extension of these associations to every city

in the United States (and, in fact, to all the cities of the world), which we predict will be very rapid, will settle the money question without legislation or civil war. We claim, therefore, that the money question is the easiest to settle, and if the forces of all whose ultimate aim is the same, namely, justice and hence the abolition of poverty, were to unite on this one reform,—the establishment of a rational money system—we could utterly destroy the money power in less than a year. Since it is this money power—*this monopoly of money*,—that has corrupted legislation, and always will as long as it lasts, it is indispensable to destroy it first, that it may not checkmate, as it always has and always will, any measure that tends to weaken its influence. *Its utter destruction, therefore, cost what it may, is the only hope for humanity.* It is needless to go any further into details to prove the paramount importance of money reform over land reform. The influence of the money power will not be denied. If for no other reason than the removal of this potential opponent of land reform, money reform and progress generally, all reformers should unite in common cause against the common enemy.

358   I cannot refrain from again calling attention, before closing this chapter, to what impresses me more and more as being the correct view in regard to the exchangeability of paper money under a true and equitable system of exchange. It is that secured credit in the form of certificates of credit, furnished in accordance with the Mutual Credit System, not being a commodity nor redeemable in a definite quantity of any commodity, is not affected by change in the value of any commodity, nor even by supply and demand as commodities are. Unlike what takes place under the "standard" money system, changes in market values or prices will not be influenced by any "money market." The medium of exchange will have no more effect on values than a pencil with which one works out a sum in arithmetic affects the result; it simply enables one to do the sum. In like manner the cer-

tificates of credit facilitate transactions, but do not affect them.   Pencils do not affect business transactions any more than the color of one's hat or necktie; neither will the certificates of credit of the Mutual Credit System.   There never can be a scarcity of secured credit any more than a scarcity of pencils.   An individual may be minus a pencil, but that is not a scarcity of pencils.   There would be a scarcity of pencils if the individual had money to exchange for one but could find no one who had any to exchange.   So likewise, secured credit would be scarce if an individual having security could not get the certificates of credit; but as long as the Mutual Credit Associations furnish them to all who can put up security, he can get them and there is no scarcity of secured credit.   If the foregoing is correct reasoning, then the certificates of credit will have no power whatever to influence values any more than a pencil or the color of one's necktie or hat has now.

359   Today money has a power, not that of facilitating exchanges, but another superadded thereto (105) and which comes from restriction, the legal tender enactment and the fact that it is a commodity and therefore affected by supply and demand.   The term "purchasing power" expresses now, not the exchangeability of money merely, but it includes this vestige of authority.   As commerce is conducted now, to buy and sell is to be engaged in a scheme to plunder.   Labor *sells* itself and money buys it.   Politicians *sell* themselves, and toilers *sell* their votes.   The tender and loving touch of woman (or what otherwise would be the magnetic and loving touch of woman) is bought and sold.   All this unholy commerce will cease under the new system.   The medium of exchange—secured credit in the form of certificates—will have no "purchasing power"; and we shall not "buy" and "sell," but *exchange*, the certificates of credit being the medium to facilitate the transfer, as the pencil is in doing the sum.   The terms buy and sell, expressing as they do transactions which are so often of a questionable character,

involving the surrender, not only of right, but of manhood
and womanhood, can hardly be terms appropriate to convey
an idea of exchange as it will be under the new system.
And the term "purchasing power." What does it signify?
It is a synonym of "Almighty Dollar"; fit contemporaries of
this age of slavery and authority. In connection with the
medium of exchange provided by the Mutual Credit System,
the term will be inapplicable. We may continue to use the
terms buy and sell, but their significance will be changed.

360 In view of existing monetary and industrial conditions, and what has been presented in this volume, what is
the need of the hour? There are those who think, or at
least affirm that they believe, that the present inexpressably
bad industrial and commercial conditions will gradually
change and we shall again see what is called "good times";
but they do not take into consideration the process that is
going on during these alternate changes,—the centralization
of wealth in the hands of a few, and the pauperization of the
masses. They fail to see that the production of wealth cannot keep pace with its absorption through compound interest
(117-126). It is folly to talk about personal effort, energy
and thrift. Everyone knows who cares to, that these qualities avail nothing of themselves. To succeed in surrounding
one's self with comforts it is necessary to be an exploiter of
men and women; to be oblivious to their sufferings; to disregard all appeals to manhood and crush out that sublime
characteristic of the most noble of our race; to stultify one's
self—turn a deaf ear to the higher criticism—and follow
only that debased and sordid ambition,—the accumulation of
a greater pile of wealth than others have been able to con-
centrate. So that to be a success, one must cultivate the
opposite of all moral teachings. And it is easily to be seen
that it is to the sufferings that many have endured rather
than become such, that we owe what little advancement and
refinement we enjoy, else the strife over mine and thine

12

would have become so fierce, that our civilization would be a still worse cannibalism than it is.

361   And to what end shall we endure all this discomfort and witness this misery? There is no rational desire that may not be fulfilled, nor luxury that may not be enjoyed by any one who is industrious under a rational system of society, the initiation of which must be preceded by a rational system of exchange. To this end, then, I proclaim the great need of the hour to be a perfect money system. We are losing time, and unless we establish such a system our children will execrate our memory—the next generation will brand us as liars and idiots; liars because we did not practice what we preached, and idiots because we deliberately defeated prosperity, and burdened it with debt.

362   Let us then briefly review The New Philosophy of Money. In what does it differ from the macaronic paralogism called "finance," or the present money muddle?

363   The former is the recognition and synthetic arrangement of all the factors that enter into the subject of the supply of money. By the proper consideration of these, principles have been discovered, and a true philosophy has been formulated.

364   The latter is the result of an unintelligent effort to attain certain ends. Principles have been disregarded, and false premises have led to erroneous conclusions.

365   In the one, the end sought is progress,—greater facilities in order to have better results with an expenditure of less labor. In the other, it is a reckless perpetuation of a system, regardless of consequences.

366   The Mutual Credit System is a plan to supply the paper medium of exchange, and has been formulated in accordance with the New Philosophy of Money. All the elements or factors pertaining thereto are recognized and duly considered. No rights are invaded, none are ignored.

367   The invention of paper money made possible the abolition of book credits by substituting it; thus making all

exchanges cash transactions. But such a revolution was not in the interest of money-lenders, as such; and although borrowers and business people interested in the change, constitute an overwhelming majority, they have never been wise enough to inaugurate it.

368 Coin, a definite quantity of commodity, being the circulating medium previous to the invention of paper money, suggested the idea of a measure of value, which gained almost universal acceptance, and has served as a pretext for limiting, through legislation, the volume of paper money proportional to the amount of the coin; thus money-lenders have reaped the advantages of this great invention for themselves alone;* the rights of borrowers and the interests of the public have been disregarded, and we have realized but a fragment of the progress we should have made had the volume of paper money been commensurate with the need for a medium of exchange.

369 Thus we see that the present system is not based on principles; that the elements or factors that pertain to the subject have never been recognized nor considered; and that, therefore, the prevailing theory of money is not a true philosophy, but is based on popular fallacy and maintained in the interest of a class.

370 The great mistake that has side tracked thought on this subject has been the notion that money-lenders are an essential factor; that we could not do without them, and that, in order to keep them within bounds of safety, we must have government control. The founder of this new philosophy, keeping right along on the main track, discovered the error

---

*The paper money of the present system is capital (30-34). That of the Mutual Credit System is credit (22, 30-34). In the former it is the credit of the money-lender (30) when it is his uncovered notes or bank bills in excess of its specie, it is true, but it always becomes capital to the borrower and the public generally. Under the latter, as just stated, it will be *credit* to the borrower and the public generally (80), because issued to the borrower direct from the printing press, and therefore neither the capital nor the credit of anyone else.

(95-95a-95b), and pointed out that co-operation, or the application of the mutual feature in the supply of money, abolishes both.

371   With regard to the volume of money under the one and the other systems, it does not take a very great effort of the intellect to realize that if all money loaned was new bills which came to the borrower direct from the printing press, notwithstanding that all of them, in their turn, would be returned to the institutions that furnished them, as the time for which they were loaned expired, the amount in circulation would largely exceed the demands of the most radical per capita Populist.   Yet such will be the case under the Mutual Credit System.   I will anticipate the exclamation on the part of the "great" financiers, political economists and money-lenders, who will pronounce this "too much money."   It will be nothing of the kind, as I shall proceed to demonstrate. "Like causes produce like effects," but different causes generally produce different effects.   The cause that produces depreciation of the paper money of the specie basis or the present system will be entirely absent under the Mutual Credit System; for that cause is the superabundance of paper issued relative to the basis on which it rests, or overissue, and hence impossibility of redemption; and no such condition can result under the Mutual Credit System, for the base is always much larger than the issue, whatever the issue may be, while the redemption of its paper money is effected in the ordinary transactions of trade.   The individual who has issued some certificates of credit furnished him by the Mutual Credit Association, is notified by the association a few days ahead, that the note which he gave in exchange for the certificates will be due on a certain day.   If he does not care to renew his note, or the security is such that the association will not extend the time for payment, he takes certificates which he has on hand or obtains by disposing of something he has for sale, proceeds to the office of the association and pays his note.   The act of taking the certificates in exchange

for whatever he sold, is the act of redemption. The return of them to the association, is the act of retiring them from circulation. The borrower must redeem a sum of money of the Mutual Credit Association equal to the amount it furnished him, and retired it from circulation. He must do it voluntarily, or the association will do it by disposing of his property.

372 The reader will see, then, that the Mutual Credit System provides a volume of money limited only by the security—any product of labor that has a market value. That it provides a most practicable and unfailing method of redemption of the money, and for its retirement from circulation.

373 The present system provides a volume of paper money equal to the quantity of gold there may be, or as much more as money-lenders and politicians are willing to take chances of being caught unable to redeem in gold. In order then, to have good money, it will necessarily have to be very scarce, and if we have plenty it will necessarily be very poor.*

374 The volume of certificates of credit in circulation will be very large compared with that of any coin basis system at any time. The low rate of interest at which it can be had, as I have shown (316,317), will induce people to use it and abandon all forms of unsecured credit. It will cost much less and be much more convenient and satisfactory, to have the ledger accounts balanced and the balances in this paper money in the safe or on deposit, than to carry them on the ledger as we do now (93-94, 308-309, 312).

375 A "great abundance" of paper money of the kind that is "redeemable in specie," causes fear of depreciation, manifesting itself in a preference for things of value. In-

---

* How strange is political economy! This delectable "science" purports to deal with, and present the correct philosophy of production and exchange; yet its theory of money is, that if we had enough of it, there would be too much!

creasing demand causes a rise in prices, which, in the case of
specie, one of the things of value, takes the form of a premium, for those who have the things of value are actuated by
the same lack of confidence.   A "great abundance" of money,
then, under such a system, means that one must pay that
much more for the goods he buys, if it does not ultimately
result in total loss.

376   We may now sum up the advantages of the Mutual
Credit System as follows: That its paper money, which is
secured credit, will take the place of *unsecured* credit, and
instead of book accounts, all transactions will be CASH, because credit in that form (paper money issued on good security) costs but a fraction of what it costs in any other form,
while its advantages are incomparably greater.

377   That it will be uniform throughout the whole
country, because all the associations that issue it will be under the supervision of one general clearing-house, and hence:

378   That it cannot depreciate in exchangeable value.

379   That it will put an end to money panics, as it can
never be scarce, because it will be issued on any product of
labor that has a market value.   That it will inaugurate a
true civilization, with prosperity exceeding anything ever
witnessed, and will, therefore, abolish poverty.

380   That it will exterminate, not only usury, but also
interest in excess of cost.

381   That under this system monopoly can have no
existence.

382   Its inauguration, then, is the one step that is needed
to free us from the grasp of the usurer, the corruption of
politics, the tyranny of superstition and creeds, the degrada-
tion of womanhood and manhood, and from all the manifold
evils that result from poverty.   In a word: It opens up to
view the true destiny of man, foreshadowing the realization
of what have been but dreams.

NOTE.

At the close of my labors on the manuscript of this work, I received from its author, Mr. Arthur Kitson, a copy of "A Scientific Solution of the Money Question. I am sorry it did not appear earlier as I should have been glad of an opportunity to quote from it. I wish, however, to express the great pleasure and profit I have derived from reading it. I consider it by far the ablest and most comprehensive treatise on the money question that I know of. Mr. Kitson is a deep thinker and a forcible writer, demonstrating his complete mastery of the subject and his familiarity with its literature.

Like myself, Mr. Kitson exposes "the great commercial fiction of the nineteenth century,"—the "measure of value," and champions the entire dissociation of government from the regulation or supply of money. With such a co-worker in the cause of liberty, one necessarily feels reassured, and a renewed hope of a speedy triumph.

APPENDIX.

It is proposed immediately to continue the work of inaugurating the Mutual Credit System suspended during the preparation of this volume, which was deemed indispensable, in order that the methods as well as the purpose of the system should be correctly and perfectly understood. Now that this is complete and given to the public, the work of procuring and enrolling membership will go on uninterruptedly until there are a sufficient number to organize the first association; the plan for which is as follows:

We, the undersigned, for the purpose of forming a Mutual Credit Association, under and by virtue of the provisions of title two (2) of chapter thirty-four (34) of the "General Statutes, 1878," of the State of Minnesota, in such case made and provided, and the laws amendatory thereof and supplementary thereto, do hereby associate ourselves together and adopt the following articles of incorporation:

ARTICLE I.

The name of this corporation shall be the Minneapolis Mutual Credit Association. The special and only business of this corporation shall be to furnish certificates of credit as provided in the articles of incorporation and by-laws. The principal place of business of this corporation shall be located in Minneapolis, Minnesota.

ART. II.

The amount of the capital stock of this corporation shall be fifty thousand dollars ($50,000), divided into five thousand shares of the par value of ten dollars each. The said stock, after the issue of the first five hundred shares, shall be sold, issued and paid in at such times as the board of directors may from time to time determine. The stock shall bear no interest nor be entitled to dividends.

ART. III.

This corporation shall commence on the ——— day of ——— 189—, and shall continue for a period of thirty years.

ART. IV.

The highest amount of indebtedness that this corporation may contract shall be ——— dollars.

ART. V.

The management of the affairs of this corporation shall be vested in a board of seven directors, a board of three appraisers, a manager, a cashier, a secretary, and a counsel at law. The manager, cashier, secretary and counsel shall be appointed by the board of directors, who shall require each to give bonds in sufficient amount to guarantee the faithful performance of their duties.

Art. VI.

As soon as five hundred shares of the capital stock shall have been subscribed for, or as soon thereafter as possible, the subscribers shall hold a meeting and elect the boards of directors and appraisers. Each subscriber shall be entitled to one vote for each share of stock, and as soon as this corporation enters upon its business of furnishing certificates, each borrower of such certificates thereby becomes a member whether a stockholder or not, and is entitled to one vote, and one additional vote for each $1,000 borrowed in excess of the first $1,000.

Art. VII.

As soon as the association is prepared to furnish certificates of credit, the stockholders shall be served first and in the order they appear on the subscription list. After all stockholders who wish to borrow, are served, anyone may obtain certificates of credit in accordance with these articles and the by-laws.

BY-LAWS OF THE MINNEAPOLIS MUTUAL CREDIT ASSOCIATION.

1   In conformity with the articles of incorporation, as soon as five hundred shares of the capital stock shall have been subscribed for, or as soon thereafter as possible, the stockholders shall hold a meeting and elect a board of seven directors and a board of three appraisers.

2   The board of directors shall appoint a manager, a cashier and a secretary, and shall require each to give bonds to the board's satisfaction, as a guarantee for the faithful performance of their duties.

3   The manager, cashier and secretary shall hold office until they resign, or are removed by the board of directors. They shall be subject to, and not members of the board, nor participate in its meetings, except when called upon to do so; and the same rule shall govern the appraisers.

4   The manager shall manage the affairs of the association, subject to the instructions of the board of directors; the cashier shall perform the usual duties, and the secretary shall have charge of all the documents, see that all mortgages are duly recorded before certificates are furnished by the association, and keep an account of the blank certificates received from the General Clearing-House Association, the disposition of the same, the cancellation of all certificates returned to the association and the transmission of all such canceled certificates to the General Clearing-House Association.

5   The board of directors shall instruct and authorize the cashier to collect an assessment upon the stock, and proceed to carry out the instructions set forth in the articles of incorporation and these by-laws; but no stockholder shall be assessed more than the par value of his stock.

6   Each subscriber to the stock shall pay fifty cents at the time he subscribes, and shall be given a receipt for the same, signed by

Alfred B. Westrup, who shall be temporary secretary; the said fifty cents to pay temporary expenses, and the same shall be considered an advance payment on the stock subscribed for.

7   The boards of directors and appraisers shall employ secretaries of their own.   The board of directors shall fix the salaries of the officers and employees, and shall employ a legal advisor, who shall be general counsel for the association, and shall pass upon the legality of all securities taken by the association.

8   The board of directors shall apply to the General Clearing-House Association as soon as it is organized, for certificates of credit of all denominations, and shall always furnish new certificates for torn or soiled ones, when requested, free of charge.

9   The board of appraisers shall first pass upon all securities before certificates are loaned by the association.

10   Any person may become a member of the association and borrow its certificates by pledging unincumbered, improved real estate, never vacant lands, situated within the corporate limits of Minneapolis, or in the immediate neighborhood thereof; or commodities not immediately perishable, and delivered to the keeping of the association.   All borrowers shall give a note for the amount furnished in certificates, but no note shall extend beyond one year, and notes secured by the more perishable commodities shall be limited in the time they are to run in proportion to the perishability of such security.   No certificates shall be loaned by the association upon any other conditions.

11   Every member of the association shall bind himself in due legal form to receive the certificates of credit issued by any of the associations that are members of the General Clearing-House Association, of which this association is a member, in payment of debt and in exchange for commodities and services, and from all persons, at their face value and without discriminating in prices.

12   Notes falling due may be renewed by the association, subject to the modification which a new valuation may require, so that there is always ample security.

13   The charge which the association shall make for the loans, and for the insurance, shall be determined by, and if possible, not exceed the cost of the same.   In case there is a surplus over expense and insurance, the same shall be paid back to the borrowers in equitable proportion; but, in order to provide for the retirement of the capital stock of the association, an extra one per cent per annum shall be charged all borrowers who are not stockholders, which assessment shall constitute a sinking fund with which the board of directors shall, from time to time, take up the capital stock and cancel the same until it is all retired; at which time this assessment shall cease.

14   Any member may, at any time, have his property released from the pledge, and be himself released from all obligations to the association, by paying his note or notes to the said association.   A stockholder who is not a borrower, may, at any time, be released from all obligations to the association by notifying the manager in writing, but thereby forfeits all right to any voice in the management of the association.

15   The association shall receive none other than its own certi-

ficates or those furnished by associations that are members of the General Clearing-House Association hereinafter mentioned. The association shall render each day a statement of its loans the day previous, describing the property pledged, giving the owner's name and its location, with the appraiser's valuation and the amount loaned on it; and also a statement of the notes paid and mortgages canceled during the same period, which statement shall be signed by the manager, cashier and secretary. A copy of each statement shall be furnished to anyone on application.

16   This association shall do all in its power to encourage the organization of similar associations in other cities, and as soon as five associations have been organized they shall proceed to organize the General Clearing-House Association, whose object shall be to provide the blank certificates of credit for the local associations, to supervise and correct any defects in the method of conducting the business, and examine the condition and management of such associations as shall adopt its prescribed rules and apply for membership prior to their being admitted, to the end that there may be uniformity in the exchangeability of such certificates throughout the whole country.

17   The General Clearing-House Association shall assume all loss from fire or otherwise to the property pledged, and also to the holders of certificates from depreciation in case of mismanagement or fraud on the part of any local association.

18   To meet the expenses of the General Clearing-House Association, and also to provide for the payment of the losses above mentioned, each local association shall contribute a percentage of the rate charged the borrower.

19   Until such time as the General Clearing-House Association shall be prepared to carry the insurance of property pledged, each association shall place its insurance in such companies as the board of directors may designate.

20   At the first meeting, the members shall determine how often and when the regular meetings of the association shall be held, make provision for calling special meetings, and how many shall constitute a quorum.

21   Each meeting shall elect a chairman and secretary, and a competent stenographer shall be employed to report the complete minutes of each meeting.

22   These by-laws may be amended at any regular meeting of the members.

EXPLANATION.

The object in forming a stock company first is to provide the funds necessary to defray the expenses of inaugurating the movement.   It is readily understood that no enterprise can be commenced without money, and this is the means taken to provide it.   It is proposed first to procure five hundred subscribers to the capital stock, and then call a meeting of the subscribers to elect the directors and other officers, incorporate, issue the first five hundred shares of the capital stock and assess the same only as funds are needed.

Instead of immediately issuing certificates of credit, it is proposed to extend the work until we have organized an association in at least five or six cities. This delay is not altogether undesirable. It will afford ample time for all the members to become thoroughly acquainted with the methods and advantages of this new system, and to study and mature the plan that shall finally be adopted; for which purpose regular meetings will be held. Each of these associations will bear its share of the expenses of carrying on the propaganda work and establishing the General Clearing-House Association. If we meet with obstacles in the way of our incorporating, we propose to keep on organizing associations until we have numbers and influence enough to remove those obstacles, whatever they may be, unless it shall be decided to proceed without incorporating, which can only be determined by a concensus of opinion. As soon as this point is settled either by having become incorporated or by deciding to proceed without incorporating, and the General Clearing-House Association having been duly organized and domiciled, it shall proceed to provide the certificates of credit and furnish them to the local associations in such denominations as they may ask for.

The General Clearing-House Association shall keep an account with each association of the blank certificates furnished it and of the mutilated and canceled ones returned. The mutilated ones being those that are presented at the office of any association as unfit for circulation, and for which new certificates are given in exchange; the canceled ones being such as are returned to the associations in payment of notes that have matured.

By organizing a number of associations and the General Clearing-House Association before any certificates are issued, we overcome the great obstacle which seems to present itself to the minds of the people as insurmountable, and which is, that a paper money will not circulate unless it is made legal tender by authority.* The New Philosophy of Money

---

* What is the meaning of the term "legal tender," as applied to money? "The Century Dictionary" defines it as "currency which can be lawfully used in paying a debt." A briefer and common definition is "compulsory circulation," and this is the term applied to such money habitually in most South American countries, *curso forzado*.

teaches that the paper medium of exchange should be good enough to be readily accepted on its merits, in which case the making of it legal tender is entirely unnecessary. By organizing five or six associations and the clearing-house, practically making them one association, before any certificates are issued, they are, when issued, acceptable by any member of any of these associations, or any that may thereafter organize and become members of the General Clearing-House Association. Now, it will hardly be denied that paper money that is acceptable by a large number of business and professional men and women in five or six cities, will also be gladly taken by any one else in those cities (except, perhaps, money-lenders), because they, also, can pay it out to those who are members of the association. It follows, also, that the enormous advantages of this system, when understood, will be the incentive to organize associations in every city. Its benefits are not confined to any locality, but are universal; if it is a good system anywhere it is good everywhere, and therefore will rapidly extend itself to all cities.

The idea of borrowing money at one or two per cent per annum is too much of a good thing to allow it to go begging. When it is known all over the country that the plan is matured and it is actually contemplated to carry it into effect, it will create more discussion than any other subject; and when it is put into practice it will create greater excitement than anything that ever happened.

There will be no need for expensive machinery to engrave plates to print the certificates from. The half-tone process will produce finer prints and facilitate greater safe-

---

Edward Atkinson, in a recent very interesting pamphlet, cites legal tender among some examples of words of which the meaning has been perverted to the vitiation of public thought, and says legal tender should be defined as "an act by which bad money may be forced into use so as to drive good money out of circulation." He has made a search through history for legal-tender acts, and concludes from his discoveries "that no decree and no statute of legal tender ever originated anywhere except for the purpose of forcing a debased coin into circulation, or for the purpose of collecting a forced loan by making paper substitutes for coin a legal tender for debts." . . . . Good money needs no act of legal tender to make it circulate. Mr. Atkinson makes an unanswerable argument on this point by citing the fact that the great international commerce of the world has been carried on from its beginning to the present time without international acts of legal tender.—*The Century, August.*

guards against counterfeiting than steel engravings possibly can.

It is asserted now without any fear that it will prove untrue, that from the start these certificates of credit will be accepted as good money anywhere. But there will be no need of sending this money off to a distance. In the first place it will not come into circulation all of a sudden, the present money disappearing as suddenly. No one will be likely to have all his customers bringing him nothing but certificates of credit, and for some time there will be a mixed currency of both the present money and the new, affording an opportunity to use the former where it may be doubtful about the acceptability of the latter. In the second place, as the certificates will be accepted by a large number of business people on the same terms as the present money, it will naturally be an easy matter to exchange the one for the other in those few cases where the individual must have the kind he does not happen to possess; and as the system extends the need of making such exchanges will become less frequent.

I am sometimes asked: "But will not the government stop you from issuing these certificates of credit?" No doubt it will try to, because it is the tool of the money power. But what of it? Shall we abandon liberty because a lot of officials take it into their heads to deprive us of it? If this system has the merits we claim for it, and if the majority can rule in this country when they decide to, it is only a question of convincing the majority of its merits to be free from government interference. In the meantime, the more government interference the more it will advertise the system and the sooner we shall get the majority on our side. Finally, if this is the only road to prosperity and happiness (and that is what we claim), we must either travel this road or give up hope and resign ourselves to the slavery we now have to endure.

It may at first appear strange to some that the stock is to bear no interest nor be entitled to dividends; but upon mature consideration they will see that this is a mutual association, and to pay interest or dividends to members of a mutual association, where the business is transacted only with members, is like taking money out of one pocket and putting it in another pocket. The object of the association is to provide that instrument of exchange which we must all use more or less, and the supply of which, in accordance with equitable principles, is indispensable to prosperity; and those who desire prosperity are asked to loan a few dollars to meet the expenses of starting the association; the same to be returned to them out of a sinking fund to be created for that purpose; so that the cost of starting will be equitably distributed.

Those who do not loan any money to the association by taking some of its stock, will have to pay a trifle higher rate of interest when they borrow. This extra charge will be set apart as the sinking fund with which the capital stock will be taken up and canceled. The association will then be purely mutual, reducing its charges to actual cost.

It is to the interest of all to facilitate the initiation of this method of supplying the medium of exchange, because it will inaugurate perpetual prosperity, and annihilate all monopoly and political knavery.

Great care has been exercised in the preparation of the foregoing plan, but it is not proposed as one that will require no modification when finally adopted; some slight changes may be found necessary in order to meet the requirements of the law, or those of an unincorporated association if such is decided upon, but which will not affect the results.

The writer, who has been an advocate of this system for twenty years, has devoted the last five to efforts for its realization, and is more hopeful than ever of its speedy accomplishment, because of the prospect that there will soon be a very thorough investigation into its merits by a large number of thinking people.

Money reform has become absolutely indispensable to save us from continued hard times or civil war, and this is the only system that will stand the test of scientific investigation.

It is very important that all who become interested in this movement should communicate at once with the secretary, and they are earnestly solicited to do so. Any criticisms or suggestions will be gratefully received, duly considered and promptly answered.

It will be necessary to publish a weekly paper to represent and defend the movement as soon as the first association is organized. This will greatly increase the opportunity for informing the people as to the object and methods of the system, which, intentionally or not, will no doubt be misrepresented.

Let the reader bear in mind that the establishment of this system means nothing less than a complete emancipation from tyranny, the inauguration of prosperity, the abolition of poverty. Not that this alone will do it, of course, but this is necessarily the first step, and will make others possible which would otherwise be impossible; even the land question (it can be demonstrated in an unanswerable manner) cannot be settled until the money question is settled. The money power and interest must be destroyed, and the Mutual Credit System is the only weapon that can do it.

It will be a great help to the cause, and facilitate propaganda work for each one in any town or city who is in favor of this money reform, to know who else in that locality is in sympathy with it. I therefore propose that each one send their name and address to me. By so doing they can be put in communication with each other. A representative of this movement is needed in every city and town in the country to organize a Mutual Credit Association. It will afford a greater opportunity for advancement than anything that anyone can engage in, and certainly none ought to be better paid, seeing that it is the most important to the human race of anything ever contemplated. Any good business man or woman can, by communicating with me, obtain all the information they need to commence to form an association, getting large remuneration as the work proceeds.

Let some one in each town and city start in at once to organize an association and get the subscribers to the capital stock; the more associations that are organizing the easier and more rapid will be the work. As soon as the General Clearing-House Association is organized and furnishing the certificates of credit, the organization of a local association will be a work of a few days. So that after it is in operation it will rapidly extend itself to every town and city, not only of this country, but of the civilized world. A movement similar to this one has already been started in London, England, called "The Free Currency Propaganda." Some of the leaders are able writers; their literature is in harmony with The New Philosophy of Money, and their work bids fair to outstrip us in results.

There are plenty of shrewd capitalists who, when they see that this system is being pushed, that it is not only to the best interest of all to establish it, but that it is inevitable, will themselves come to the front and help inaugurate it.